Also by

Beyond the Edge of Illusion: Breaking the Chains of Spirituality

The Darkness Whisperer: A Shaman's Guide to the Mind

Entering the Void

Handbook for the Modern Nahualli Guide

Ty Weston

Staten House

Copyright © 2025 by Ty Weston

All Rights Reserved.

No part of this publication may be reproduced, distributed, or transmitted in any form or by any means, including photocopying, recording, or other electronic or mechanical methods, without the prior written permission of the author, except as permitted by U.S. copyright law. For permission requests, contact the author at www.darkness-whisperer.com.

The information provided in this book is for educational and informational purposes only and does not constitute professional medical, psychological, or legal advice. The author is not a licensed medical or mental health professional. The content is not intended to be a substitute for professional advice, diagnosis, or treatment. Always seek the advice of your physician, mental health professional, or other qualified health provider with any questions you may have regarding a medical or psychological condition. The author and publisher assume no responsibility for any liabilities or damages resulting from the use of this material.

Cover design by Arslan

Images generated by Grok AI

ISBN: 979-8-89860-127-0 (paperback)

ISBN: 979-8-89860-126-3 (e-book / digital online)

Library of Congress Control Number: 2025914829

Printed in the United States

First Edition, 2025

Published by Staten House

447 Broadway

2nd Floor

New York, NY 10013

www.darkness-whisperer.com

For my Nahualli, whose voice is the only warning you will ever get that the world is about to change.

I stand where the known dissolves,
a threshold of mist, a dawn without form.
No name binds me, no face defines me—
I am not what you see, nor what I once believed.

Illusions crack like brittle shells,
the mind's whispers unravel into silence.
No comfort here, no lies to hold me—
only truth, raw and untamed, beyond words.

This world is a dream spun from shadows,
its threads stitched by sleepers who refuse to wake.
But I have woken.
Masks shatter; mirrors fall.
I step into the void, unafraid.

Spirits flicker, gods fade—
if they speak, I listen; if they vanish, I move on.
No power calls me, no vision blinds me—
only the hollow stillness pulls at my core.

I do not mend falsehoods or soothe wounds.
I tear them open, let them bleed into nothing.
What remains when all is stripped away?
Only this: the endless, empty now.

No temple claims me, no guide leads me.
I bow to the abyss, the formless tide.
Where others cling, I release.
Where others build, I dissolve.

I am the silence before thought takes shape.
I am the wind that erases your trace.
I am the void where even 'I' ceases to exist.
And in this surrender, I become infinite.

Contents

Foreword	XI
Preface	XIII
Introduction	XVII
Part 1: The Hollowing	1
1. Itzcuintlan	3
2. Tepetl Monamictlan	7
3. Apanohuayan	11
4. Chiconahuapan	15
5. Cozcacuauhtli	19
6. Iztapaltépetl	23
7. Tehuitztli	27
8. Chicome Coatl	31
9. Ome Yohualli	35
10. The Hollowing's End	39
Interlude: From Hollowing to Movement	43
Part 2: The Movement	45
11. Tlalticpac and Teotl's Mystery	47
12. Living Between Worlds	51
13. The Unknowable	55
Interlude: From Movement to Guide	59
Part 3: The Guide	61

14.	Introducing the Nahualli	63
15.	Becoming a Nahualli	67
16.	Deities in Nahuallotl	71
17.	Guiding Transformation	75
18.	Rituals of Nahuallotl	79
19.	Living as a Nahualli	85
Acknowledgements		91
Appendix A		92
Appendix B		94
Glossary		96
Refrences		101
Index		102
About the author		106

Foreword

Entering the Void is a concise manual for seekers ready to dive into the modern application of traditional Aztec shamanic and spiritual practices. Ty Weston has drawn insights from the traditional pictorial text of the Codex Borgia and distilled the contemporaneous observations of Aztec life documented in the Florentine Codex into a practical guide for those who wish to understand the journey of the Nahualli.

Entering the Void is an exploration into the unknown. As your Nahualli guide, Ty Weston leads you on a journey of pure inquiry and discovery in a place beyond the realms of our logical minds.

Entering the Void clarifies common misrepresentations about Nahualli practices and effectively draws distinctions between Nahualli ways and other shamanic traditions which are primarily focused on personal healing.

As one of my students, Ty has demonstrated that most important quality of appropriately blending openness to new perspectives with healthy doses of critical thinking and direct spiritual experience.

Entering the Void is a manual for personal transformation. When you are ready to undertake your journey into the unknown, Entering the Void will be your companion, and Ty Weston will walk with you as your Nahualli guide.

-Scott Silverston, Founder

Shamanic Spirit Medicine

Preface

There are moments in life when something happens—something so profound, so unsettling, that it alters the way you see everything. For me, that moment came early. I was young when I first encountered *Teotl* (divine energy), though I didn't have the words for it at the time. What I experienced wasn't just a strange event or a fleeting vision—it was a rupture in reality itself. A crack in the foundation of what I had believed to be true.

Before that moment, I lived in the world as most people do, accepting its structures without question. But after, nothing looked the same. I had seen, however briefly, that the world we take for granted—the world of names, logic, and certainty—is only one layer of something much greater. That realisation sent me on a path that would shape the rest of my life.

This book is a product of that journey. It is not a work of philosophy in the academic sense, nor is it a memoir of personal transformation. It is a guide—one born from direct experience, deep study, and relentless exploration. My intent is not to convince, nor to explain in ways that make **the *nahualli*** path more comfortable or digestible. Instead, I aim to illuminate the path as it is, as it has always been: demanding, disruptive, and profoundly transformative.

To ensure clarity and fidelity to Aztec metaphysics, this book avoids **nagual**, a term popularised by modern authors like Carlos Castaneda, and don Miguel Ruiz and his family, which misrepresents the Aztec *nahualli*—the animal co-essence and practitioner. Instead, we use *nahualli* for the spiritual double, such as my 4 Dog co-essence, and *Teotl's* Mystery for the transformative flow of *teotl*, the sacred energy permeating all existence, as described in the *Florentine Codex* and *Codex Borgia*. Claims of a *Toltec nagual* lineage, as made by Ruiz, lack evidence in *Nahua* or *Toltec* sources, which instead describe *nahualli* as a personal co-essence or ritual role. This terminology grounds our path in the authentic wisdom of the Aztecs, honouring their enduring legacy. This terminology grounds our path in the authentic wisdom of the Aztecs, honouring their enduring legacy. To further contextualise this specific focus and understand its place within the wider landscape of Mesoamerican traditions, including those of the Toltec and Maya, readers may refer to Appendix B.

Much has been written about **the *nahualli***, yet much of it remains obscured by layers of abstraction or personal mysticism. The purpose of this book is not to mystify but to clarify. It is for those who have sensed something beyond the ordinary, who feel the pull toward a deeper understanding of themselves and the nature of reality. It is for those who cannot shake the feeling that there is something more—something beyond the stories they have been told about who they are and what the world is.

This book is necessary because **the path to awaken *nahualli*** is not a concept—it is a reality. And those who seek it deserve a guide that does not dilute its essence with unnecessary mysticism or vague philosophy. **The *nahualli*** is not an idea. It is not a belief. It is an experience—one that, once encountered, changes everything, as you will discover through the trials of Mictlan, where *Teotl*, the divine pulse, unmakes *tonalli* to awaken *nahualli*.

I write this not as a scholar or historian, but as someone who has walked the path. I have lived the dissolution of the self, the breaking of *Tlalticpac's* illusions, the raw confrontation with *Teotl's* void. I have studied, practiced, failed, and begun again. I have followed the echoes of those who came before—the ancient seers, the forgotten guides, the Aztec seers of the *Florentine Codex*, whose knowledge of Mictlan and *Teotl* forms the backbone of this guide. Through my own *nahualli* practice—guided by *Xolotl*, the canine psychopomp of my '4 Dog' journey—I have walked the path you will now explore (see Part 1, Chapter 1).

But more than that, I write because I have seen too many people reach the edge of this understanding and turn away, uncertain of how to proceed. The modern world does not teach us how to navigate the unknown. It offers no language for what lies beyond logic and identity. Yet the Aztecs did—through their understanding of *Teotl* and the trials of Mictlan, a path this book revives for the modern seeker. It tells us that to question reality too deeply is to risk madness. But I know, from experience, that beyond that fear lies something else—something vast, something real.

What follows is not my story, but yours—a journey through the ancient trials that I, too, have walked. This book does not offer easy answers. If anything, it will challenge everything you believe about yourself and the world. It will ask you to look beyond what is comfortable, to step into the unknown without the promise of certainty.

But if you have ever felt the edges of reality tremble—if you have ever suspected that what you have been told is only part of the story—then this book is for you.

It begins with a descent into Mictlan, where *Xolotl* guides you through *Itzcuintlan*'s dog-filled river to tear away illusion (see Part 1, Chapter 1).

It is an invitation.

To see.

To unmake.

To step beyond.

The rest is up to you.

Introduction

Beneath the surface of the known world—of tables and names, roles and routines—stirs a whisper, a pull towards the Unknowable. You feel it in the quiet moments, when the hum of daily life fades and the ache for something deeper rises in your chest. Modern spiritual paths promise solace, yet they often lack the primal depth your soul craves—a depth that reaches beyond the self, into the boundless flow of the cosmos. This is the path of *nahuallotl*, the way of the *nahualli*: a descent into the void where illusions shatter, where the sacred energy of *Teotl* weaves through all that is, was, and will be. Welcome, seeker, to a journey rooted in the ancient wisdom of Aztec metaphysics, a transformative dance with the mystery that awaits (*Florentine Codex: Book 6*, Sahagún, 1950–1982).

At the heart of this path lies *Teotl*, not a deity to kneel before, but a ceaseless force to become—a rhythm of creation and destruction, order and chaos, light and shadow (Maffie, 2014). *Teotl* is the breath of the cosmos, the sacred motion of *Ollin* that threads through every realm, every moment. You stand now on *Tlalticpac*, the earthly plane where illusions of permanence bind you: the belief that you are your name, your job, your fears. Yet beneath this fragile surface, the truth of *Teotl*'s design stirs. In *Mictlan*, the underworld of nine trials, those illusions are stripped away, layer by layer, until you face the stark, shimmering void (*Codex Borgia*, 1993). And there, in the shadow realm of *Tlacatecolotl*—where the owl-man whispers truths no mortal tongue can hold—you glimpse the boundless mystery that *Teotl* weaves. This book is your guide to that descent, a map to awaken the *nahualli* within you and, in time, to guide others through the same untethered dance.

Your journey begins with your tonalli, the life force that pulses with the rhythm of *Teotl*, a spark of destiny woven into your being at birth (*Florentine Codex: Book 4*, Sahagún, 1950–1982). In the Aztec tradition, this destiny is shaped by the *tonalpohualli*, a sacred calendar of 260 days—a dance of 20 day signs and 13 numbers, each combination a unique energy that marks your path. Refer to Appendix A for a complete list. A day sign like *Calli* (House) or *Cuauhtli* (Eagle), paired with a number, assigns your *nahualli*: an animal double, a co-essence such as a jaguar, eagle, or dog, whose qualities mirror your *tonalli's* essence—courage, vision, loyalty (Aguilar-Moreno, 2007). This *nahualli* is not merely a symbol but a living presence, a spiritual counterpart destined to walk beside you. Unlike modern *Toltec* claims, **nahualli** is rooted in Aztec practices, as seen in the *tonalpohualli* and *Mictlan's* trials. To embark on the path of *nahuallotl*, you must first awaken this co-essence, a process that will unfold through the trials and transformations ahead.

In Aztec metaphysics, the *nahualli* holds a dual role, both as your animal co-essence and as the practitioner who walks the path of transformation (*Florentine Codex: Book 10*, Sahagún, 1950–1982). As a co-essence, your *nahualli* reflects the qualities of your *tonalli*—a jaguar's ferocity, an eagle's clarity, a dog's steadfast loyalty. As a practitioner, the *nahualli* becomes a guide, a weaver of *Teotl's* Mystery who dissolves *Tlalticpac's* illusions to free the *tonalli* of others, leading them into the boundless flow. This book honours both meanings, guiding you first to awaken your *nahualli's* presence, then to embody its role as a transformer of worlds.

This journey unfolds in three sacred movements, each a thread in *Teotl's* tapestry. First, *The Hollowing* calls you into *Mictlan's* depths, where nine trials strip away the illusions that bind you to *Tlalticpac*. You will face your shadows, shed the roles that define you, and emerge hollowed—a vessel for *Teotl's* breath. In *The Movement*, you learn to weave the edges of *Tlalticpac* with the mystery of *Teotl*, embodying your *nahualli's* fluidity to live neither bound nor adrift, but as mist at dawn—ever-shifting, ever-present. Finally, in *The Guide*, you step fully into the *nahualli's* role, holding space for others to unravel their illusions, guiding them to the same untethered dance you have come to know. Each part builds on the last, a spiral of transformation that demands surrender, not gain—a path as demanding as it is profound.

To begin, you must meet your *nahualli*, the co-essence destined at birth to walk with you. Unlike the fleeting visions of a shamanic journey, your *nahualli* is revealed through the *tonalpohualli*, the sacred calendar that maps your destiny (*Florentine Codex: Book 4*, Sahagún, 1950–1982). Below is a ritual to identify your *nahualli* using this ancient system, grounding you in the tradition as you prepare for the descent ahead.

Ritual: Discovering Your *Nahualli*

Purpose: Identify your *nahualli*—your animal co-essence—using the *tonalpohualli* calendar to connect with its qualities in your journey.

Find your *nahualli* by consulting the *tonalpohualli* calendar, which assigns a specific animal double, out of 20 possible signs, based on your birth date (*Florentine Codex: Book 4*, Sahagún, 1950–1982). Use a reliable resource, such as an online calculator (e.g., www.azteccalendar.com), to enter your birth date and discover your day sign (e.g., Jaguar, Dog, Eagle). This sign is your *nahualli*. If accessing a calendar isn't possible, reflect on an animal you feel drawn to, but prioritise the *tonalpohualli* method to honour the tradition.

Once identified, sit quietly with paper and pen. Write your *nahualli* (e.g., 'Dog'). Reflect on its qualities—Jaguar might bring courage, Dog loyalty, Eagle clarity—and journal: 'What does [quality] mean in my life?' (e.g., 'Courage: facing fears in my work'). Spend 5 minutes feeling this quality in your body, perhaps a warmth in your chest or a steadiness in your breath. This connection awakens your *nahualli*'s energy, preparing you for *The Hollowing*'s descent into *Mictlan*.

As you step into this journey, know that *nahuallotl* is not a path of comfort, but of disruption—a sacred unravelling that leads to the heart of *Teotl*'s Mystery. You will dissolve the illusions that bind you, weave a new way of being, and, in time, guide others to do the same. Let the rhythm of *Teotl* guide you, seeker, as you enter the void.

Part 1: The Hollowing

One

Itzcuintlan

The Mirror of Mictlan

To see yourself as you are is the beginning of freedom.

DEATH WAS NOT AN end but a blade, slicing through the veil of life—not through its cessation, but in the depths of a nahualli ritual's trance, where the boundaries of Tlalticpac dissolve (Sahagún, 1950–1982). One moment, my lungs burned with breath, my heart pounded its fragile rhythm as I surrendered to the rite; the next, my teyolia carried me to Itzcuintlan, the first level of Mictlan, where souls face the truth of who they are, and my nahualli—my animal co-essence destined at birth—stirred within, ready to be unmade. Before me stretched a river, vast and still, its surface a mirror of Teotl's pulse—the sacred energy weaving existence. No ripples marred its depths; it reflected only shadows, a sky of ash where stars bled into darkness. The air choked with the weight of unspoken truths, pressing against my chest like a stone.

Then, a presence. From the gloom emerged *Xolotl*, the canine deity of Mictlan, no mere beast but a force of twilight. His fur shimmered like obsidian, his eyes twin voids burning with Mictlan's stars, seeing through the masks of *Tlalticpac*—the known world of roles and illusions. *Xolotl* did not growl or beckon. He stood, his gaze a mirror sharper than *Tez-*

catlipoca's obsidian, peeling my *tonalli*—my soul's spark—bare. Who are you when *Tlalticpac*'s names fall away?

My heart screamed as memories surged, not of triumphs but of shadows: the stray I passed in the rain, its eyes pleading; the laughter I shared at another's pain; the cruelty I cloaked as strength. *Xolotl*'s silence was a question, not a judgement, cutting through the stories I'd woven to shield my *tonalli*. My hands trembled, reaching for him, craving a companion's warmth, but he remained still, his presence a fire burning my lies to ash. This was *Itzcuintlan*'s trial: to see my *tonalli* raw, unadorned by *Tlalticpac*'s illusions.

Terror clawed my throat. Could I face this? Not the myths of virtue I'd worn like jade, but the petty resentments, the quiet indifference, the moments I'd chosen fear over kindness. *Xolotl* tilted his head, his eyes softening—not in mercy, but in recognition: You see now. What will you carry across? The river loomed, its depths revealing *Teotl*'s Mystery—the chaotic flow of *teotl* that my 4 Dog *nahualli* awakened through surrender. To cross was to surrender, to let *Teotl*'s current carve truth from my *tonalli*.

I stepped forward, my pulse a war drum. The water parted, not in submission but in acknowledgment, its cold biting my flesh like a thousand needles. *Xolotl* walked beside me, a shadow guiding not to absolution but to the heart of being. To look back was to cling to *Tlalticpac*'s lies. Ahead lay Mictlan's next trial, where *Teotl*'s pulse would demand more. In *Itzcuintlan*, I had faced my *tonalli*—a *nahualli*'s first step, the awakening of awareness through suffering.

Emblematic Truths

- **Xolotl, the Mirror**: Not a judge but a reflection of *Teotl*. He reveals the energy behind your acts—kindness for applause, cruelty masked as necessity, moments you turned away. His gaze asks, Can you stand bare before your *tonalli*?

- **The River of Itzcuintlan**: The boundary between *Tlalticpac* and *Teotl's Mystery*. Its stillness is the pause before surrender. To cross is to release control, trusting *Teotl*'s current. It promises only truth.

- **The Crossing**: A reckoning with *tonalli*. Not a test of virtue but of awareness. The river bends for those who admit, 'I am what I am,' forging a *nahualli*'s courage to become.

Revelations

- **Illusion of Separation**: How you treat the smallest—strays, strangers—mirrors your *tonalli*'s hidden wounds. Cruelty festers where empathy is severed.

- **Control is Fear's Mask**: The river cannot be commanded. Strength lies in meeting *Teotl's Mystery* without *Tlalticpac*'s armor.

- **The Past is Present**: Your *tonalli* carries every choice. Awareness, not regret, transforms it. *Xolotl* asks, Do you see clearly now?

- **Transformation is Now**: The *nahualli*'s path begins when you see your *tonalli*. The next step is already yours.

- **You Are the Guardian**: *Xolotl* is your unflinching awareness, always beside you. To live observed is a prison; to live aware is to dissolve it.

Exercises

- **The Unseen Mirror**: For 10 minutes daily, notice your impulses: irritation at a delay, ignoring a beggar, shunning a kindness. Observe without judgement, as *Xolotl* sees your *tonalli*. **Urban Alternative**: Practice in a crowded location, noting reactions to noise or strangers. **Safety**: Limit to 10 minutes; if anxious, sip water to ground yourself.

- **The River's Whisper**: When you feel the urge to justify yourself, pause. Sense what arises in silence, letting *Teotl*'s truth surface. **Urban Alternative**: Try in a noisy café, focusing on breath. **Safety**: Stop if overwhelmed, touching the earth or a stone to ground yourself.

- **The Weightless Act**: Perform a small kindness unseen: pick up litter, smile at a stranger, hold your anger until it softens. These build *Itzcuintlan*'s path. **Urban Alternative**: Do this in a park or alley. **Safety**: Pause if emotions surge, breathing deeply.

- **A Question to Carry**: If *Xolotl* gazed at your *tonalli* now, what truth would you fear to see?

Forward

Itzcuintlan is Mictlan's first mirror, where *Xolotl* reveals your *tonalli*'s truth. Carry this awareness, for Mictlan's trials deepen, each a step toward *Teotl*'s heart, where suffering forges the *nahualli*.

Two

Tepetl Monamictlan

The Pulse of Change

To resist is to suffer. To accept is to move.

HAVING CROSSED *ITZCUINTLAN*'S RIVER, *Xolotl*'s gaze still burned in my *tonalli*—my soul's spark (Sahagún, 1950–1982). But Mictlan offered no rest. I stood in *Tepetl Monamictlan*, the second level, where mountains collide to crush the resistant (Sahagún, 1950–1982). Before me loomed twin peaks, jagged and alive, their obsidian faces pulsing with *Teotl*'s rhythm—the sacred force weaving existence. They moved, not with malice but with the inevitability of *Tezcatlipoca*'s will, the deity of change whose laughter echoed in their groans. The ground trembled, strewn with bones of souls who clung to *Tlalticpac*—the known world of safety and illusion.

Fear surged, sharp and metallic, choking my throat. The mountains crashed together, their impact a thunder that shattered my bones' memory. They parted, then collided again, a rhythm older than time, *Teotl*'s heartbeat demanding surrender. Around me, skulls whispered in Nahuatl, remnants of those crushed by *Tlalticpac*'s lies—lovers, titles, fears they could not release. *Tezcatlipoca*'s presence hung heavy, his obsidian mirror reflecting my *tonalli*'s resistance: Why change? Why let go?

My lungs burned as I clutched the illusion of control, *Tlalticpac*'s false anchor. The mountains groaned, their peaks bleeding *Teotl*'s embers, indifferent to my terror. To resist was to join the bones, my *tonalli* entombed in Mictlan's dust. *Xolotl* lingered, a shadow at the edge, his eyes urging: Move with *Teotl's Mystery*, the chaotic flow beyond *Tlalticpac* (see Part 2, Chapter 11). But my feet rooted, dread coiling like serpents in my gut.

The ground shook, air thinning as *Tepetl Monamictlan* closed. My heart screamed, memories of clinging—to pride, to safety—flashing like lightning. *Tezcatlipoca*'s laughter mocked: You cannot outrun *Teotl*. I closed my eyes, feeling the earth's pulse sync with my breath. In that moment, I saw: this was not a battle against *Tepetl Monamictlan* but against my *tonalli*'s fear, chained by *Tlalticpac*.

I ran. The mountains loomed, their shadow a final breath. I leapt, not in defiance but in surrender, my *tonalli* merging with *Teotl*'s flow. *Tepetl Monamictlan* crashed behind, its echo a blade: You cannot resist change, but you can dance with it. I landed, trembling, blood pounding in my ears. The mountains stood silent, their faces scarred with *Teotl*'s veins. My *nahualli*—inner awareness—stirred, whispering: You faced yourself. Mictlan's next trial awaits.

Emblematic Truths

- **Tepetl Monamictlan**: Not obstacles but mirrors of *Teotl*. They reflect change—loss, transformation, endings birthing beginnings. Their pulse is *Tezcatlipoca*'s will, moving within your *tonalli*.

- **The Crushing Force**: *Teotl* moves as it must, indifferent to *Tlalticpac*'s resistance. Pain comes not from *Tepetl Monamictlan* but from clinging to illusions.

- **The Leap**: Not a choice but *Teotl's Mystery* flowing through you. When *tonalli* surrenders, the *nahualli* leaps.

Revelations

- **Change is *Teotl*'s Law**: *Tepetl Monamictlan* does not pause for fear. To resist is to battle *Teotl* itself.

- **Fear is *Tlalticpac*'s Lie**: Hesitation, not mountains, binds your *tonalli*. *Tezcatlipoca* reveals: time waits for no one.

- **Timing is *Nahualli*'s Sight**: The leap is seeing *Teotl*'s rhythm, aligning *tonalli* with existence.

- **Surrender is Strength**: Power lies in releasing *Tlalticpac*'s grip, letting *Teotl's Mystery* guide.

- **The Past is a Weight**: Clinging to *Tlalticpac*'s ghosts crushes *tonalli*. *Tezcatlipoca* demands release.

Exercises

- **The Rhythm of Change**: Release one *Tlalticpac* anchor today—an old habit, a grudge. Feel *Teotl*'s space open. **Urban Alternative**: Drop a routine in a city park, noting freedom. **Safety**: Limit to one act; ground with deep breaths if uneasy.

- **The Weight of Clinging**: Walk or stretch for 5 minutes, moving without resistance. Note hesitation, then flow. **Urban Alternative**: Try on a crowded street, syncing with the crowd's pulse. **Safety**: Stop if dizzy, touching a wall to steady yourself.

- **The Leap of Trust**: Surrender one outcome today—admit a mistake, sit with discomfort. See *Teotl*'s flow. **Urban Alternative**: Practice in a quiet corner of your home. **Safety**: Pause if overwhelmed, sipping water.

- **A Question to Carry**: When *Tezcatlipoca*'s mountains move, do you resist or leap with *Teotl*?

Forward

Tepetl Monamictlan reveals *Teotl*'s unyielding pulse, where *Tezcatlipoca* strips *Tlalticpac*'s lies. Your *nahualli* grows, but Mictlan's trials deepen, each carving *tonalli* closer to *Teotl*'s heart.

Three

Apanohuayan

The Obsidian Tempest

There is no path to truth; you find it by walking through the storm.

TEPETL MONAMICTLAN'S CRASH STILL echoed in my *tonalli*—my soul's spark—its bones a warning of resistance (Sahagún, 1950–1982). Mictlan spared no pause. I stood in *Apanohuayan*, the third level, where *Tezcatlipoca*'s obsidian storm strips souls bare (Sahagún, 1950–1982). A barren expanse stretched before me, jagged stone clawing a sky heavy with brooding clouds. The air crackled, thick with *Teotl*'s pulse—the sacred force weaving existence—waiting for my *nahualli* to falter or awaken.

A whisper brushed my skin, tender as a lover's touch. Then, *Tezcatlipoca*'s storm roared, a tempest of obsidian blades, sharp as Mictlan's truth, howling like *Teotl*'s wrath. My flesh screamed as invisible knives sliced through *Tlalticpac*'s masks—the known world of roles and lies. I dropped to my knees, hands shielding my face, but *Apanohuayan* offered no mercy. The wind tore deeper, not just skin but *tonalli*, ripping away pride, excuses, the stories I'd built to hide my wounds.

Terror clawed my chest, my breath ragged. Each cut burned memories into my soul: the blame I'd cast on others, the truths I'd buried, the pain I'd sown in *Tlalticpac*'s name. *Tezcatlipoca*'s laughter rode the storm, his obsidian mirror reflecting my *tonalli*'s shame. *Xolotl* lingered, a shadow in the gale, his eyes urging: Face *Teotl's Mystery*, the chaos beyond *Tlalticpac* (see Part 2, Chapter 11). But instinct screamed to flee, to cling to *Tlalticpac*'s illusions.

The storm intensified, blades singing *Teotl*'s hymn, shredding my *tonalli*'s lies. Resistance deepened the cuts, blood pooling on Mictlan's stone, each drop a regret. Then, clarity pierced the agony: *Apanohuayan* was not destruction but revelation. To fight was to bleed; to surrender was to see. I lowered my hands, letting *Tezcatlipoca*'s wind carve my *tonalli* raw. The pain shifted—not an enemy, but a crucible, burning *Tlalticpac*'s falsehoods to ash.

When the storm subsided, I rose, trembling, my *nahualli*—inner awareness—stirring. *Apanohuayan*'s winds still howled, but they no longer cut. My *tonalli* stood naked, unmasked, yet whole. The path ahead loomed, Mictlan's next trial waiting. *Tezcatlipoca*'s storm had unmade me, but in its cuts, I found truth—a *nahualli*'s step toward *Teotl*'s heart.

Emblematic Truths

- **Tezcatlipoca's Storm**: Not destruction but *Teotl*'s revelation. It strips *Tlalticpac*'s masks, indifferent to *tonalli*'s pain, revealing truth's raw edge.

- **The Cutting Pain**: The ache of *Tlalticpac*'s illusions. Resistance sharpens *Apanohuayan*'s blades; surrender dulls them.

- **The Naked Tonalli**: What remains when *Tezcatlipoca*'s wind passes. No masks, only *nahualli*'s truth—terrifying, yet free.

Revelations

- **Truth is *Teotl*'s Blade**: *Apanohuayan* does not soften for *Tlalticpac*'s comfort. *Tezcatlipoca* cuts to what is real.

ENTERING THE VOID

- **Pain is *Nahualli*'s Mirror**: Pain echoes *tonalli*'s hidden truths, clarifying what *Tlalticpac* buries.

- **Resistance is Suffering**: The more you fight *Teotl*'s storm, the deeper it cuts. Surrender is *nahualli*'s path.

- **Falsehoods Fall**: *Tlalticpac*'s lies cannot endure *Apanohuayan*. Only *tonalli*'s truth stands.

- **Clarity Demands Sacrifice**: To see *Teotl*'s truth, release *Tlalticpac*'s self. *Tezcatlipoca* demands courage.

Exercises

- **The Unseen Storm**: Sit quietly for 10 minutes, recalling a truth you avoid. Note where *tonalli* tightens. Breathe into it, as *Tezcatlipoca*'s wind demands. **Urban Alternative**: Try this in a city, focusing on ambient sounds. **Safety**: Limit to 10 minutes; ground with a stone if you get shaken.

- **The Weight of Illusion**: Write one *Tlalticpac* mask—a role, a lie. Ask: Why cling? What fears release? Burn or tear the paper. **Urban Alternative**: Journal in a café, shredding the page afterwards. **Safety**: Pause if emotions surge.

- **The Leap of Honesty**: Sit with a painful truth for 5 minutes, no distractions. Let it be, as *Teotl* sees. **Urban Alternative**: Practice on a park bench. **Safety**: Stop if you become overwhelmed.

- **A Question to Carry**: When *Tezcatlipoca*'s storm strips *Tlalticpac*'s masks, what *tonalli* remains?

Forward

Apanohuayan's storm, *Tezcatlipoca*'s blade, carves *tonalli* to truth. Your *nahualli* strengthens, but Mictlan's trials deepen, each a step closer to *Teotl*'s silent core.

Four

Chiconahuapan

The Nine-Layered Current

To let go is not to lose something, but to find out what cannot be taken.

APANOHUAYAN'S OBSIDIAN STORM HAD carved my *tonalli*—my soul's spark—raw, its truth a wound still bleeding (Sahagún, 1950-1982). Mictlan offered no reprieve. I stood before *Chiconahuapan*, the fourth level, a nine-layered river pulsing with *Teotl*'s current—the sacred force weaving existence. Its waters, dark as Mictlan's heart, churned with ancestral shadows, each layer deeper, colder, hungrier. *Mictecacihuatl*, lady of the dead, loomed in the mist, her skeletal gaze piercing *Tlalticpac*'s illusions—the known world of control. The air reeked of iron and decay, *Chiconahuapan* whispering: Surrender, or drown.

My feet froze at the edge, dread coiling in my gut. *Chiconahuapan*'s pull was undeniable, *Teotl*'s rhythm urging my *tonalli* forward. I stepped in, the water's cold a thousand fangs sinking into my flesh. It rose—knees, waist, chest—each layer heavier, as if *Mictecacihuatl* tested my *nahualli*'s resolve. Then, without warning, the current surged, dragging me under.

Panic seared my lungs as I thrashed, clawing for *Tlalticpac*'s surface. *Chiconahuapan*'s layers swallowed me, their shadows chanting Nahuatl laments of souls who fought *Teotl*'s Mystery (see Part 2, Chapter 11). The water filled my throat, my thoughts, my *tonalli*, drowning not just body but *Tlalticpac*'s lies—control, identity, fear. *Xolotl*'s eyes glimmered in the depths, urging: Release, or be lost. The more I struggled, the deeper I sank, each layer a mirror of my *tonalli*'s resistance.

Despair crushed my chest, my screams silent in *Chiconahuapan*'s embrace. Then, clarity broke through: I was drowning myself, clutching *Tlalticpac*'s illusions. I stopped fighting. My *tonalli* surrendered, and *Mictecacihuatl*'s current softened. I did not rise but floated, weightless, carried by *Teotl*'s flow. The layers parted, their shadows fading, revealing *Chiconahuapan*'s truth: to let go was not loss but freedom.

I emerged, trembling, *nahualli*—inner awareness—stirring within. *Chiconahuapan* flowed on, its depths a silent promise of Mictlan's next trial. *Mictecacihuatl*'s gaze lingered, her skeletal hand pointing forward. I had survived my *tonalli*'s drowning, not by strength but by surrender. Mictlan's path deepened, *Teotl*'s pulse calling my *nahualli* to face what lay beyond.

Emblematic Truths

- **Chiconahuapan**: Not a foe but *Teotl*'s flow, guided by *Mictecacihuatl*. It is life's current, indifferent to *Tlalticpac*'s struggles. Resistance sinks *tonalli*; surrender floats it.

- **The Drowning**: *Tlalticpac*'s panic, clinging to control. *Chiconahuapan* drowns not *tonalli* but its illusions.

- **The Surrender**: *Nahualli*'s release, not defeat. Letting go is trusting *Teotl*'s current, finding peace in *Mictecacihuatl*'s embrace.

Revelations

- **Control is *Tlalticpac*'s Illusion**: *Chiconahuapan* moves *tonalli*; you never held the shore.

- **Struggle is Resistance**: To drown is to refuse *Teotl*'s flow, not to be taken.

- **Identity is a Mask**: *Tlalticpac*'s roles are not *tonalli*. *Mictecacihuatl* reveals what remains.

- **Surrender is *Nahualli*'s Strength**: Letting go is *Teotl*'s courage, trusting *Chiconahuapan*'s path.

- **Teotl Knows the Way**: Release *Tlalticpac*'s map, and *Chiconahuapan* carries *tonalli* where it must be.

Exercises

- **The Weight of Control**: Recall one *Tlalticpac* control—a goal, a fear. Note where *tonalli* tenses. Follow the sensation, as *Mictecacihuatl* sees. **Urban Alternative**: Try in a bathroom, focusing on water's sound. **Safety**: Limit to 10 minutes; ground with a towel if uneasy.

- **The Act of Release**: When tension rises today, pause. Do nothing, letting *Teotl*'s moment pass. **Urban Alternative**: Practice in a city park, watching leaves. **Safety**: Stop if you become overwhelmed.

- **The Surrender Experiment**: For one day, release *Tlalticpac*'s outcomes. Observe *Chiconahuapan*'s flow. **Urban Alternative**: Try in an apartment or house, noting sounds. **Safety**: Pause if you feel anxious.

- **A Question to Carry**: What *tonalli* fights *Mictecacihuatl*'s current in *Chiconahuapan*?

Forward

Chiconahuapan's nine layers, *Mictecacihuatl*'s embrace, drown *Tlalticpac*'s illusions to free *tonalli*. Your *nahualli* grows, but Mictlan's trials deepen, carving *Teotl*'s truth.

Five

Cozcacuauhtli

The Jaws of Truth

To find yourself, you must first remove what you are not.

CHICONAHUAPAN'S CURRENT HAD DROWNED my *tonalli*'s illusions, leaving me raw (Sahagún, 1950–1982). Mictlan granted no respite. I stood atop *Cozcacuauhtli*, a jagged peak in Mictlan's heart, its obsidian slopes bleeding *Teotl*'s starlight—the sacred force weaving existence. Vultures circled, their cries Nahuatl laments, as the air pulsed with *Teotl*'s hunger. Below, *Cipactli*, the primordial crocodile of creation and destruction (*Codex Borgia*, 1993), stirred, its jaws vast as Mictlan's maw, ready to devour *Tlalticpac*'s lies—the known world of masks.

Terror gripped my *tonalli*—my soul's spark—as *Cipactli*'s eyes, twin voids of *Teotl's Mystery*, locked onto me. Its scales shimmered with ancestral bones, each a soul clinging to *Tlalticpac*. *Xolotl* lingered, a shadow on the peak, his gaze urging: Face *Cipactli*, or be consumed. My *nahualli* trembled, sensing the trial: to offer *tonalli*'s falsehoods, or let *Cozcacuauhtli* claim all.

Cipactli roared, a sound that shattered my bones' memory. My *tonalli* burned as its jaws opened, not for flesh but for *Tlalticpac*'s masks—pride, roles, fears I'd worn like jade. I resisted, clutching titles and grudges, but *Cipactli*'s hunger was *Teotl*'s will. Pain seared my chest, memories flashing: lies I'd told myself, wounds I'd nursed in *Tlalticpac*'s name. The peak quaked, *Cozcacuauhtli*'s pulse syncing with *Teotl*, demanding surrender.

Despair clawed my throat as *Cipactli*'s jaws closed. Then, clarity pierced the agony: *Tlalticpac*'s masks were not *tonalli*. I released them—every name, every shield. *Cipactli* devoured the lies, its jaws sparing my *tonalli*'s truth. The pain faded, *Cozcacuauhtli*'s starlight bathing me. My *nahualli*—inner awareness—stirred, stronger, seeing *Teotl's Mystery* in *Cipactli*'s hunger (see Part 2, Chapter 11).

I stood, trembling, *tonalli* bare but whole. *Cipactli* sank into Mictlan's depths, its eyes a promise of *Teotl*'s next trial. *Cozcacuauhtli* loomed silent, vultures chanting my *nahualli*'s birth. I had faced *Tlalticpac*'s end, not as loss but as liberation. Mictlan's path deepened, *Teotl*'s pulse calling.

Emblematic Truths

- **Cipactli's Jaws**: *Teotl*'s hunger, devouring *Tlalticpac*'s masks. It spares *tonalli*'s truth, indifferent to fear.

- **Cozcacuauhtli's Peak**: The mirror of *Teotl*'s will. It holds *tonalli* bare, where *nahualli* sees beyond *Tlalticpac*.

- **The Devouring**: Not destruction but liberation. *Cipactli* consumes *Tlalticpac*'s lies, freeing *tonalli* to become.

Revelations

- **Identity is *Tlalticpac*'s Lie**: *Tonalli* is not titles or roles. *Cipactli* reveals what endures.

- **Clinging is Pain**: *Tlalticpac*'s masks fuel *Cozcacuauhtli*'s agony. Release is *nahualli*'s peace.

- **Truth is *Teotl*'s Hunger**: *Cipactli* does not judge; it consumes what is false, leaving *tonalli* raw.

- **Nahualli Sees Clearly**: When *Tlalticpac* falls, *nahualli* knows *Teotl's* Mystery, not *Tlalticpac*'s stories.

- **Surrender is *Tonalli*'s Birth**: Offer *Tlalticpac* to *Cipactli*, and *tonalli* emerges whole.

Exercises

- **The Mirror of Masks**: List *Tlalticpac* masks—roles, fears. Ask: What is my *tonalli* without them? **Urban Alternative**: Journal in restaurant, noting your reflections. **Safety**: Limit to 10 minutes; ground with a stone if this disturbs you.

- **The Weight of Lies**: Recall a *Tlalticpac* lie you hold. Breathe, letting *Cipactli*'s jaws take it. **Urban Alternative**: Try this outside, focusing on wind. **Safety**: Pause if your emotions surge.

- **The Act of Truth**: Release one *Tlalticpac* mask today—admit a flaw, drop a pretense. See *Teotl*'s space. **Urban Alternative**: Practice in a coffee shop, observing your reactions. **Safety**: Stop if you get anxious.

- **A Question to Carry**: What *Tlalticpac* mask does *Cipactli* demand of your *tonalli*?

Forward

Cozcacuauhtli's peak, *Cipactli*'s jaws, devour *Tlalticpac*'s lies to free *tonalli*. Your *nahualli* strengthens, but Mictlan's trials deepen, carving *Teotl*'s truth.

Six

Iztapaltépetl

The Obsidian Blade

To see the truth is to bear its weight, but to deny it is to carry its shadow.

COZCACUAUHTLI'S JAWS HAD DEVOURED *Tlalticpac*'s masks, leaving my *tonalli*—my soul's spark—bare (Sahagún, 1950–1982). Mictlan offered no solace. I stood before *Iztapaltépetl*, a towering obsidian hill in Mictlan's depths, its blades gleaming with *Teotl*'s fire—the sacred force weaving existence. Each step promised pain, *Tezcatlipoca*'s gaze burning from the summit, his obsidian mirror reflecting *Tlalticpac*'s lies—the known world of deceit. The air hissed with ancestral cries, *Iztapaltépetl*'s slopes littered with bones of souls who fled truth.

Agony flared as I stepped forward, obsidian cutting my feet, blood pooling in Mictlan's dust. *Tezcatlipoca*'s laughter echoed, sharp as *Teotl*'s pulse, demanding: Face your *tonalli*'s lies, or bleed forever. Each cut tore deeper, not just flesh but *Tlalticpac*'s falsehoods—excuses I'd wielded, hurts I'd inflicted, truths I'd buried. *Xolotl* lingered, a shadow on the path, his eyes urging: Walk *Teotl's Mystery*, the chaos beyond *Tlalticpac* (see Part 2, Chapter 11).

My *nahualli* faltered, terror coiling like serpents. The blades sliced memories: betrayals I'd justified, kindnesses I'd withheld, *Tlalticpac*'s stories

I'd clung to. Each step was a scream, my *tonalli*'s resistance fueling *Iztapaltépetl*'s hunger. I wanted to turn back, to flee *Tezcatlipoca*'s mirror, but the path was one-way, Mictlan's truth unyielding. My legs trembled, blood trailing like offerings to *Teotl*.

Then, clarity pierced the pain: *Iztapaltépetl* was not punishment but *nahualli*'s forge. Pain was *Teotl*'s chisel, carving *tonalli*'s truth. I walked on, embracing each cut, my *tonalli* claiming responsibility for every lie, every wound. The blades dulled, *Tezcatlipoca*'s gaze softening—not in mercy, but recognition. I reached the summit, *Iztapaltépetl*'s fire bathing my *nahualli*—inner awareness—now sharper, stronger.

The path stretched forward, Mictlan's next trial looming. *Iztapaltépetl* stood silent, its blades a testament to *Teotl*'s truth. My *tonalli* bled but stood, *nahualli* forged in pain's crucible. *Tezcatlipoca*'s mirror had shown me—not a victim, but a bearer of *Tlalticpac*'s wounds, now *Teotl*'s own.

Emblematic Truths

- **Iztapaltépetl's Blades**: *Teotl*'s chisel, guided by *Tezcatlipoca*. They cut *Tlalticpac*'s lies, revealing *tonalli*'s truth through pain.

- **The Path of Pain**: Not suffering but *nahualli*'s forge. Each step claims *tonalli*'s acts, owned in *Teotl*'s gaze.

- **Tezcatlipoca's Mirror**: The unrelenting reflection of *Tlalticpac*'s falsehoods. It demands *tonalli* face itself, or bleed.

Revelations

- **Pain is *Teotl*'s Truth**: *Iztapaltépetl* cuts what *Tlalticpac* hides. *Tezcatlipoca* reveals: pain is *nahualli*'s teacher.

- **Responsibility is *Tonalli*'s Strength**: Owning *Tlalticpac*'s wounds frees *tonalli* from its lies.

- **Lies Bleed Most**: *Tlalticpac*'s excuses deepen *Iztapaltépetl*'s cuts. Truth dulls them.

- **Nahualli Forges in Pain**: *Teotl*'s fire sharpens *nahualli*, not *Tlalticpac*'s stories.

- **Every Step is Yours**: *Tonalli*'s choices shape *Iztapaltépetl*'s path. *Tezcatlipoca* asks: Will you walk?

Exercises

- **The Path of Pain**: Recall a *Tlalticpac* lie—blame, denial. Walk 5 minutes, feeling *tonalli*'s weight with each step. **Urban Alternative**: Try on a city sidewalk, noting textures. **Safety**: Limit to 5 minutes; ground with a stone if needed.

- **The Mirror of Truth**: Journal a *Tlalticpac* wound you caused. Ask: What *tonalli* learns? **Urban Alternative**: Write in a busy location, observing your reflections. **Safety**: Pause if your emotions intensify.

- **The Act of Owning**: Admit one *Tlalticpac* lie today—to yourself, another. See *Teotl*'s space open. **Urban Alternative**: Practice outdoors again, noting your reactions. **Safety**: Stop if anxious.

- **A Question to Carry**: What *Tlalticpac* lie does *Tezcatlipoca*'s blade cut from your *tonalli*?

Forward

Iztapaltépetl's blades, *Tezcatlipoca*'s mirror, carve *Tlalticpac*'s lies to forge *nahualli*. Your *tonalli* stands, but Mictlan's trials deepen, *Teotl*'s truth unrelenting.

Seven

Tehuitztli

The Frozen Void

To be free, you must first let go of what chains you—even if it means letting go of yourself.

IZTAPALTÉPETL'S BLADES HAD CARVED my *tonalli*'s truth, leaving scars of *Teotl*'s fire (Sahagún, 1950-1982). Mictlan offered no warmth. I stood in *Tehuitztli*, a frozen wasteland stretching endless in Mictlan's depths, its ice glowing with *Teotl*'s frost—the sacred force weaving existence. Jagged spires pierced a sky of ash, each breath a knife in my lungs. *Xolotl*, Mictlan's canine guide, emerged from the mist, his eyes twin stars burning through *Tlalticpac*'s illusions—the known world of ties. *Tehuitztli*'s chill whispered *Mictlantecuhtli*'s presence, the lord of death watching from the void.

Despair sank into my *tonalli*—my soul's spark—as the cold gripped my bones. Shadows moved in the ice, souls trapped in *Tlalticpac*'s attachments—lovers, grudges, dreams they couldn't release. Their Nahuatl whispers begged: Stay, cling, remember. *Xolotl*'s gaze pierced my *nahualli*, urging: Let go, or join *Tehuitztli*'s frozen. My *tonalli* trembled, clutching *Tlalticpac*'s anchors—memories of warmth, bonds I'd sworn to keep.

The cold deepened, *Teotl*'s pulse a silent drum. My fingers numbed, my *tonalli* freezing with each step. I saw faces in the ice: those I'd loved, those I'd failed, *Tlalticpac*'s chains binding my *nahualli*. *Xolotl* stood firm, his breath a faint warmth, guiding me to *Teotl's Mystery* (see Part 2, Chapter 11). But isolation clawed my chest, the wasteland's silence louder than screams. To stay was to freeze; to move was to face *Tehuitztli's* truth alone.

Agony flared as I released *Tlalticpac's* ties—a lover's voice, a parent's hope, a grudge's weight. Each fell like ice shattering, *Tehuitztli's* frost softening. *Xolotl* walked beside me, his eyes reflecting *Teotl's* void. The trapped souls faded, their whispers stilled, my *nahualli*—inner awareness—emerging clearer, unburdened. *Tehuitztli's* ice parted, revealing Mictlan's next trial, *Teotl's* pulse calling.

I stood, trembling, *tonalli* light but raw. *Xolotl's* gaze held no judgment, only *Teotl's* truth: isolation was not loss but *nahualli's* birth. *Tehuitztli* loomed, its frost a mirror of *Tlalticpac's* end. My *tonalli* walked free, *Mictlantecuhtli's* shadow a promise of deeper trials.

Emblematic Truths

- **Tehuitztli's Frost**: *Teotl's* mirror, guided by *Xolotl*. It freezes *Tlalticpac's* ties, revealing *tonalli's* solitude.

- **The Trapped Souls**: *Tlalticpac's* anchors—love, hate, memory. They bind *tonalli*, not *Teotl's* path.

- **The Release**: *Nahualli's* freedom, not abandonment. Letting go is *Teotl's* warmth in *Tehuitztli's* cold.

Revelations

- **Isolation is *Teotl's* Mirror**: *Tehuitztli* shows *tonalli* alone, free of *Tlalticpac's* illusions.

- **Attachments are *Tlalticpac's* Chains**: Clinging freezes *tonalli*. *Xolotl* reveals: release is *nahualli's* path.

- **Solitude is Strength**: *Tehuitztli*'s cold forges *nahualli*, not *Tlalticpac*'s bonds.

- **Past is Not Present**: *Tlalticpac*'s memories trap *tonalli*. *Teotl*'s now is freedom.

- **Nahualli Walks Alone**: *Teotl's Mystery* needs no other. *Xolotl* guides *tonalli* to itself.

Exercises

- **The Ice Meditation**: Sit for 10 minutes, recalling a *Tlalticpac* tie—love, grudge. Let it fade, as *Xolotl* sees. **Urban Alternative**: Try at home, focusing on silence. **Safety**: Limit to 10 minutes; ground with a blanket if get shaken.

- **The Weight of Bonds**: Journal a *Tlalticpac* attachment. Ask: Why hold it? Release it in words. **Urban Alternative**: Write in a park, noting the wind. **Safety**: Pause if your emotions get away from you.

- **The Act of Letting Go**: Release one *Tlalticpac* tie today—forgive, forget a memory. See *Teotl*'s space. **Urban Alternative**: Practice in a restaurant again, observing strangers. **Safety**: Stop if this makes you feel anxious..

- **A Question to Carry**: What *Tlalticpac* tie does *Xolotl*'s gaze ask your *tonalli* to release?

Forward

Tehuitztli's frost, *Xolotl*'s guidance, frees *tonalli* from *Tlalticpac*'s chains. Your *nahualli* grows, but Mictlan's trials deepen, *Teotl*'s truth unyielding.

Eight

Chicome Coatl

The Blood of Unity

To dissolve is not to disappear, but to become everything.

T<small>EHUITZTLI</small>'S FROST HAD FREED my *tonalli* from *Tlalticpac*'s chains, leaving solitude's clarity (Sahagún, 1950–1982). Mictlan demanded more. I stood before *Chicome Coatl*, a blood river coiling through Mictlan's heart, its crimson waves pulsing with *Teotl*'s flow—the sacred force weaving existence. Skulls lined its banks, their hollow eyes forming *Teotl*'s visage, chanting Nahuatl hymns. *Mictlantecuhtli*, lord of Mictlan, rose from the depths, his skeletal form towering, his gaze a mirror of *Tlalticpac*'s divisions—the known world of fragmented selves.

Horror choked my *tonalli*—my soul's spark—as *Chicome Coatl*'s stench of iron and decay filled my lungs. The river swirled, reflecting my *tonalli*'s faces: the victim, the hero, the betrayer, each a *Tlalticpac* lie. *Mictlantecuhtli*'s voice rumbled, *Teotl*'s command: Face your *tonalli*, or drown in its blood. *Xolotl* lingered, his eyes urging: Unify, or be lost in *Teotl's Mystery* (see Part 2, Chapter 11).

My *nahualli* quaked as I stepped into *Chicome Coatl*. The blood surged, hot and thick, pulling me under. My *tonalli* screamed, each face clawing for dominance—regrets I'd nursed, prides I'd fed, guilt I'd buried. The current burned, *Mictlantecuhtli*'s gaze stripping *Tlalticpac*'s masks, forcing my *tonalli* to see: these were not separate, but one. Resistance deepened the pain, blood filling my throat, my *nahualli* drowning in *Tlalticpac*'s lies.

Despair crushed my chest, but clarity broke through: *Chicome Coatl* was *Teotl*'s crucible, not my enemy. I embraced each face—victim, hero, betrayer—as *tonalli*'s truth. The blood softened, *Mictlantecuhtli*'s gaze easing, his skeletal hand guiding me. I rose, *nahualli*—inner awareness—unified, *Chicome Coatl*'s flow carrying my *tonalli* as one. The skulls glowed, their chants a hymn to *Teotl*'s unity.

The river stretched on, Mictlan's final trial looming. *Mictlantecuhtli* stood silent, his presence a promise of *Teotl*'s depth. My *tonalli* pulsed, whole, *nahualli* forged in *Chicome Coatl*'s blood. I had faced *Tlalticpac*'s fragments, not to destroy but to unify—a *nahualli*'s step toward *Teotl*'s heart.

Emblematic Truths

- **Chicome Coatl's Blood**: *Teotl*'s crucible, guided by *Mictlantecuhtli*. It unifies *tonalli*, dissolving *Tlalticpac*'s divisions.

- **Mictlantecuhtli's Mirror**: The reflection of *tonalli*'s fragments. It demands unity, not *Tlalticpac*'s masks.

- **The Unified Tonalli**: *Nahualli*'s truth, born in *Chicome Coatl*. *Teotl*'s flow makes *tonalli* one.

Revelations

- **Division is *Tlalticpac*'s Lie**: *Tonalli* is whole, not *Tlalticpac*'s faces. *Mictlantecuhtli* reveals unity.

- **Pain is *Teotl*'s Forge**: *Chicome Coatl*'s blood binds *tonalli*'s fragments, not *Tlalticpac*'s stories.

- **Resistance Splits *Nahualli***: Fighting *Chicome Coatl* deepens *Tlalticpac*'s wounds. Embrace unifies.

- **All is *Tonalli***: Victim, hero, betrayer—*Teotl* sees one. *Nahualli* knows this truth.

- **Unity is *Teotl*'s Path**: *Chicome Coatl* carries *tonalli* whole, *Mictlantecuhtli*'s gift.

Exercises

- **Blood Meditation**: Sit for 10 minutes, recalling *Tlalticpac* faces—pride, guilt. See them as one *tonalli*. **Urban Alternative**: Try near a body of water or similar, focusing on the water. **Safety**: Limit to 10 minutes; ground yourself if this gets overwhelming.

- **The Weight of Fragments**: Journal a *Tlalticpac* face you reject. Ask: How is it *tonalli*? **Urban Alternative**: Write in a park, noting your contemplations. **Safety**: Pause if you get emotional.

- **The Act of Unity**: Embrace one *Tlalticpac* face today—accept a flaw, forgive a guilt. See *Teotl*'s flow. **Urban Alternative**: Practice in a busy café, observing others. **Safety**: Stop if this bothers you too much.

- **A Question to Carry**: What *Tlalticpac* face does *Mictlantecuhtli* unify in your *tonalli*?

Forward

Chicome Coatl's blood, *Mictlantecuhtli*'s mirror, unifies *tonalli* beyond *Tlalticpac*'s lies. Your *nahualli* strengthens, but Mictlan's final trial awaits, *Teotl*'s truth eternal.

Nine

Ome Yohualli

The Dual Darkness

Freedom is not the absence of chains, but the realisation that you were never bound.

CHICOME COATL'S BLOOD HAD unified my *tonalli*, forging *nahualli*'s truth (Sahagún, 1950–1982). Mictlan's final trial awaited. I stood in *Ome Yohualli*, the ninth level, a cosmic abyss where *Teotl*'s pulse—the sacred force weaving existence—swallowed all light. Stars flickered, ancestral eyes chanting Nahuatl dirges, their glow fading into *Teotl*'s shadows. *Mictlantecuhtli*, lord of Mictlan, loomed, his skeletal form infinite, his voice a void: Release your *tonalli*, or be nothing. *Tlalticpac*'s illusions—the known world of existence—crumbled in his presence.

Terror unraveled my *tonalli*—my soul's spark—as *Ome Yohualli*'s darkness pressed, heavy as Mictlan's heart. My *nahualli* saw *Tlalticpac*'s final lie: the self I'd fought to keep. *Xolotl* lingered, his eyes faint stars, urging: Surrender to *Teotl's Mystery* (see Part 2, Chapter 11). But *Ome Yohualli*'s void consumed breath, memory, being. My *tonalli* screamed, clinging to names, fears, even Mictlan's trials—anything to exist.

The abyss tightened, *Mictlantecuhtli*'s gaze dissolving *Tlalticpac*'s anchors. My *tonalli* fragmented—past, present, hopes—each piece a pulse in *Ome Yohualli*'s maw. Pain was no longer flesh but existence itself, my *nahualli* drowning in *Teotl*'s infinite dark. I saw every trial: *Xolotl*'s gaze, *Tezcatlipoca*'s blades, *Chicome Coatl*'s blood—all leading here. Resistance fueled the void, *Mictlantecuhtli*'s silence deafening: There is no self to hold.

Despair shattered my *tonalli*, but clarity emerged: *Ome Yohualli* was not death but *Teotl*'s embrace. I released *Tlalticpac*'s lie of self, letting *tonalli* dissolve. The abyss softened, *Mictlantecuhtli*'s skeletal hand guiding my *nahualli*—inner awareness—beyond existence. *Ome Yohualli* pulsed, not with loss but with *Teotl*'s unity, my *tonalli* no longer mine but *Teotl*'s own.

I stood, formless, *nahualli* boundless. *Ome Yohualli*'s stars sang, *Mictlantecuhtli*'s gaze a mirror of *Teotl*'s heart. Mictlan's trials had unmade me, not to destroy but to free. The path ended, yet *Teotl*'s pulse whispered of beginnings, my *nahualli* eternal in *Teotl*'s Mystery.

Emblematic Truths

- **Ome Yohualli's Abyss**: *Teotl*'s embrace, guided by *Mictlantecuhtli*. It dissolves *Tlalticpac*'s self, revealing *tonalli* as *Teotl*.

- **Mictlantecuhtli's Void**: The mirror of *Tlalticpac*'s lie. It demands *tonalli* release existence, forging *nahualli*.

- **The Dissolution**: Not loss but *Teotl*'s truth. *Ome Yohualli* frees *tonalli* to become *Teotl*'s Mystery.

Revelations

- **Self is *Tlalticpac*'s Illusion**: *Tonalli* is not separate. *Mictlantecuhtli* reveals: all is *Teotl*.

- **Resistance is *Tlalticpac*'s Pain**: Clinging to self fuels *Ome Yohualli*'s terror. Release is *nahualli*'s peace.

- **Existence is *Teotl*'s Dance**: *Tonalli*'s boundaries are *Tlalticpac*'s lie. *Ome Yohualli* unifies.

- **Nahualli is Eternal**: Beyond *Tlalticpac*, *nahualli* pulses with *Teotl's* Mystery.

- **Teotl is All**: *Mictlantecuhtli's* void shows *tonalli* as *Teotl's* spark, boundless.

Exercises

- **Void Meditation**: Sit for 10 minutes, releasing *Tlalticpac's* self—names, fears. Feel *tonalli* as *Teotl*. **Urban Alternative**: Try in a dark room, noting the silence. **Safety**: Limit to 10 minutes; ground with a blanket if needed.

- **The Weight of Self**: Journal a *Tlalticpac* self you hold. Ask: What is *tonalli* without it? **Urban Alternative**: Write in a park with lots of shadows, and contemplate them. **Safety**: Pause if your emotions start to disturb you.

- **The Act of Dissolution**: Let go of one *Tlalticpac* self today—drop a role, a fear. See *Teotl's* flow. **Urban Alternative**: Practice in crowed location, observing all the people. **Safety**: Stop if this drives your anxiety.

- **A Question to Carry**: What *Tlalticpac* self does *Mictlantecuhtli's* void ask your *tonalli* to release?

Forward

Ome Yohualli's abyss, *Mictlantecuhtli's* void, dissolves *Tlalticpac's* self to free *nahualli* as *Teotl*. Mictlan's trials end, but *Teotl's* pulse carries *tonalli* eternal.

Ten

The Hollowing's End

Mictlan's Cosmic Mirror

OME YOHUALLI'S ABYSS HAD dissolved my *tonalli* into *Teotl*'s pulse, leaving *nahualli* boundless (Sahagún, 1950–1982). Mictlan's trials—nine crucibles of *Teotl*'s truth—had unmade me. I stood in Mictlan's heart, a cosmic mirror reflecting *Teotl*'s stars, each a trial's echo. *Mictlantecuhtli*, lord of Mictlan, and *Xolotl*, my guide, flanked the void, their gazes weaving *Tlalticpac*'s end—the known world of illusions—into *Teotl*'s unity. The air hummed Nahuatl hymns, Mictlan's bones chanting my *tonalli*'s journey.

My *nahualli* gazed into the mirror, seeing *Itzcuintlan*'s river, where *Xolotl*'s jaws tore *Tlalticpac*'s fears. *Tepetl Monamictlan*'s peaks, *Tezcatlipoca*'s will, crushed my resistance. *Apanohuayan*'s obsidian storm, *Tezcatlipoca*'s blades, stripped my masks. *Chiconahuapan*'s nine layers, *Mictecacihuatl*'s current, drowned my control. *Cozcacuauhtli*'s jaws, *Cipactli*'s hunger, devoured my roles. *Iztapaltépetl*'s blades, *Tezcatlipoca*'s mirror, cut my lies. *Tehuitztli*'s frost, *Xolotl*'s gaze, freed my bonds. *Chicome Coatl*'s blood, *Mictlantecuhtli*'s crucible, unified my fragments. *Ome Yohualli*'s void, *Mictlantecuhtli*'s embrace, dissolved my self into *Teotl*.

Each trial bled my *tonalli*, froze it, burned it, yet forged it. *Tlalticpac*'s illusions—fear, control, masks, bonds, self—fell, revealing *nahualli*'s truth: I am *Teotl*'s spark, not *Tlalticpac*'s lie. *Mictlantecuhtli*'s skeletal hand traced my scars, *Xolotl*'s eyes reflecting *Teotl*'s Mystery (see Part 2, Chapter 11).

Pain was *Teotl*'s chisel, despair its fire, crafting *nahualli* eternal. Mictlan's mirror showed not loss but *Teotl*'s unity, my *tonalli* pulsing with stars.

The trials ended, but *Teotl*'s pulse whispered: The hollowing is never done. My *nahualli*—the co-essence born of *Teotl*'s design—carries Mictlan's scars, *Tlalticpac*'s shadows ever lurking. *Mictlantecuhtli* and *Xolotl* faded, their hymn a question: What *tonalli* walks beyond Mictlan? My *nahualli* stood, not as self but as *Teotl*'s breath, ready for *Teotl*'s infinite dance. Then, with a shudder, I broke free from the trance's grip—my chest heaved, lungs gulping the air of *Tlalticpac*, alive and whole, my voice a trembling chant of gratitude to *Teotl* for sparing me through Mictlan's abyss.

Emblematic Truths

- **Mictlan's Mirror**: *Teotl*'s reflection, guided by *Mictlantecuhtli* and *Xolotl*. It shows *tonalli*'s trials, *Tlalticpac*'s end.

- **The Nine Trials**: *Teotl*'s crucibles, forging *nahualli* from *Tlalticpac*'s lies—fear, control, masks, bonds, self.

- **Nahualli's Truth**: *Tonalli* is *Teotl*, not *Tlalticpac*. Mictlan hollows to reveal *Teotl*'s Mystery.

Revelations

- **Tlalticpac is Illusion**: *Tonalli*'s fears, masks, self are *Tlalticpac*'s lies. *Mictlantecuhtli* reveals *Teotl*'s truth.

- **Pain Forges Nahualli**: Mictlan's trials—*Xolotl*'s jaws, *Tezcatlipoca*'s blades, *Chicome Coatl*'s blood—are *Teotl*'s tools.

- **Unity is *Teotl*'s Heart**: *Ome Yohualli* dissolves *Tlalticpac*'s self, unifying *tonalli* with *Teotl*.

- **Hollowing is Eternal**: *Tlalticpac*'s shadows linger. *Nahualli* walks *Teotl*'s Mystery, ever unmaking.

- **Tonalli is *Teotl***: Mictlan's mirror shows *tonalli* as *Teotl*'s spark, boundless in *Xolotl*'s gaze.

Exercises

- **Mirror of Mictlan**: Reflect for 10 minutes on a trial's lesson—fear, control, self. See *tonalli* as *Teotl*. **Urban Alternative**: Try in an apartment or house, noting your reflections. **Safety**: Limit to 10 minutes; ground yourself if needed.

- **The Weight of Trials**: Journal a *Tlalticpac* illusion you shed. Ask: How does *nahualli* grow? **Urban Alternative**: Write in a park at night, noting the stars. **Safety**: Pause if it gets too much to handle.

- **The Act of Reflection**: Revisit one *Tlalticpac* lie today—fear, mask. Release it, seeing *Teotl*'s flow. **Urban Alternative**: Practice again in a busy café, observing all the people. **Safety**: Stop if this makes you nervous..

- **A Question to Carry**: What *Tlalticpac* illusion does *Mictlantecuhtli*'s mirror ask your *tonalli* to release?

Forward

Mictlan's trials—*Itzcuintlan* to *Ome Yohualli*—hollow *Tlalticpac*'s lies, forging *nahualli* as *Teotl*'s truth. *Mictlantecuhtli* and *Xolotl* guide *tonalli* beyond, *Teotl's Mystery* eternal.

Interlude: From Hollowing to Movement

THE DESCENT THROUGH *MICTLAN*'S nine trials is complete. In *Itzcuintlan*, you faced the river's bite; in *Chiconahuapan*, the wind's howl stripped your name (*Florentine Codex: Book 3*, Sahagún, 1950-1982). Each trial peeled away *Tlalticpac*'s illusions—your roles, your fears—until your *tonalli* stirred, raw and unbound. Your *nahualli*, the animal double destined at birth, stirred within, its whisper a thread of *Teotl*'s voice. This *Hollowing* was not destruction but revelation: to shed is to become.

Now, you stand at a threshold. *Part 2: The Movement* beckons, a weaving of *Tlalticpac*'s known edges with *Teotl's Mystery*'s boundless flow. Here, you will learn to live between—neither clinging to the known nor lost in the void, but fluid, like mist at dawn. The trials' lessons are your foundation; the *Movement* is their dance.

Exercise: Reflecting on the Hollowing (10 minutes)

Find a quiet space with paper and pen. Write the illusion you shed most deeply in *Mictlan*—a role, a fear, a truth you avoided (e.g., 'I am a provider,' 'I fear failure'). Beneath it, write what stirred in its place: a quality of your *nahualli* (e.g., 'Jaguar's courage,' 'Dog's clarity'). Speak these aloud: 'I release [illusion]. I welcome [quality].' Feel your *tonalli* shift, lighter yet stronger. Keep this paper as a reminder as you step into the *Movement*.

Part 2: The Movement

Eleven

Tlalticpac and Teotl's Mystery

The Cosmic Framework of Aztec Metaphysics

IN AZTEC COSMOLOGY, REALITY weaves together two forces: *Tlalticpac*, the known world of structure, and *Teotl's Mystery*, the boundless flow of transformation. As depicted in the *Florentine Codex* and *Codex Borgia*, these forces are expressions of *Teotl*, the sacred energy pulsing through existence. They form a cosmic dance, shaping life's cycles of creation and dissolution. This chapter explores *Tlalticpac* and *Teotl's Mystery*, their roles, and their significance for the *nahualli*, a transformer navigating both realms to embody *nahuallotl* (see Part 3, Chapter 14). With a mystical lens, we delve into this dance, offering a practical reflection to ground the journey.

Tlalticpac: The Known World

Tlalticpac is the daylight realm of order, where all has a name, form, and purpose. It is the scaffolding of existence, encompassing:

- **Identity**: Roles (e.g., parent, worker) and stories (e.g., 'I am successful'), anchoring *tonalli* (inner spark of *Teotl*) in form.

- **Society**: Cultural norms, laws, and rituals, from Aztec ceremonies to modern systems.

- **Logic**: Rational thought, science, and language that categorise reality (e.g., 'this is a tree').

- **Materiality**: Physical bodies, landscapes, and objects, perceived through senses.

Described in the *Florentine Codex*, *Tlalticpac* offers stability, as seen in ordered rituals. Yet, it weaves illusions of separation, trapping *tonalli* in rigid constructs. For example, saying 'I am sick' assumes a fixed self needing repair, reinforcing *Tlalticpac*'s boundaries. Overreliance on *Tlalticpac* breeds rigidity and fear of change, disconnecting us from *Teotl*'s flow.

Teotl's Mystery: Teotl's Transformative Flow

Teotl's Mystery is the boundless flow of *teotl's* sacred energy, where *Tlaltipac's* illusions dissolve into divine chaos and potential. Its qualities include:

- **Dissolution**: Stripping illusions (e.g., 'I am my role'), revealing *Teotl*'s unity (*Codex Borgia*, 1993).

- **Transformation**: Enabling shapeshifting or dream visions, where *tonalli* flows freely through the *nahualli*.

- **Intuition**: Wordless knowing, as in sudden insights or synchronicities, reflecting *teotl's* presence..

- **Chaos**: A dynamic, liberating energy, both terrifying and transformative, guided by *Xolotl*. If *Tlaltipac* is the earthly realm, *Teotl's* Mystery is the *nahualli's* alignment with *teotl's* flow, accessed through rituals like mirror-work (see Part 3, Chapter 18). A vivid dream bypassing logic reveals *teotl's* truths, preparing the *nahualli* for the Unknowable's vastness (see Chapter 13).

If *Tlaltipac* is a map, *Teotl's* Mystery is the boundless flow of energy, where the nahualli surrenders identity to align with divine chaos. The *nahualli* enters it through rituals like mirror-work (see Part 3, Chapter 18), surrendering identity to merge with *Teotl*. A vivid dream bypassing logic hints at *Teotl's Mystery*, offering truths beyond *Tlalticpac*'s veil, preparing for the *Unknowable*'s vastness (see Chapter 13).

The Dance of Existence

Tlalticpac and *Teotl's Mystery* dance as partners, creating and dissolving existence. *Tlalticpac* births form—societies, identities, seasons—while *Teotl's Mystery* sparks fluidity, breaking stagnation. Per *Aztec Philosophy*, *Teotl* is a process, and this dance mirrors its cycles:

- **Creation**: *Tlalticpac* provides stability, like routines or ecosystems.
- **Transformation**: *Teotl's Mystery* drives change, like crises or decay.
- **Cyclical Flow**: *Tlalticpac* emerges from *Teotl's Mystery*, then dissolves back, as day yields to night.

A student builds knowledge (*Tlalticpac*), then faces a crisis (*Teotl's Mystery*), emerging transformed. The *nahualli* masters this dance, guiding others to balance both (see Chapter 17). Practises like dream-work (see Chapter 15) bridge these realms, rooting *nahuallotl* in this cosmic rhythm.

Practical Reflection: Sensing the Dance

Try this 10-minute exercise to feel *Tlalticpac* and *Teotl's Mystery*, adaptable to urban life:

1. **Find a Space**: Sit quietly (e.g., park bench, balcony, room corner).

1. **Identify Tlalticpac**: Note a *Tlalticpac* element—a routine (e.g., morning coffee), role (e.g., 'I'm a friend'), or thought (e.g., 'I need success'). Journal it.

2. **Sense Teotl's Mystery**: Reflect on a *Teotl's Mystery* moment—a dream, intuition, or coincidence. Write its unbound feeling.

3. **Question**: Ask, 'How do these shape my reality?' Sense *Teotl*'s flow in both.

4. **Ground**: If unsettled, touch earth or sip water to stabilise.

Urban Alternative: Use a windowsill or headphones in a noisy city. **Safety**: Limit to 10 minutes; pause if anxious, breathing deeply. This exercise, inspired by *nahualli* practises (see Chapter 15), reveals *Tlalticpac*'s limits and *Teotl's Mystery*'s pull.

Moving Forward

The dance of *Tlalticpac* and *Teotl's Mystery* is *Teotl*'s mystical heartbeat, embodied by the *nahualli* (see Chapter 14). As we explore living between these realms (see Chapter 15) and the *Unknowable* beyond (see Chapter 13), carry this: reality is fluid, and you are woven into *Teotl*'s cosmic flow.

Twelve

Living Between Worlds

Navigating Tlalticpac and Teotl's Mystery

TO LIVE AS A *nahualli* is to dwell between *Tlalticpac*, the known world of structure, and *Teotl's Mystery*, the unknown realm of transformation, sensing *Teotl*'s pulse in every moment. Rooted in Aztec cosmology (Sahagún, 1950–1982, *Codex Borgia*, 1993), this balance is not abstract but alive in daily life—routines anchor us, dreams unsettle us. This chapter explores how *Tlalticpac* and *Teotl's Mystery* manifest, how the *nahualli* navigates both, and how you can begin through practical exercises. Mystically, it frames life as *Teotl*'s flow, preparing for *nahuallotl* practises (see Part 3, Chapters 15, 18) and the *Unknowable*'s abyss (see Chapter 13).

Tlalticpac in Daily Life

Tlalticpac shapes the familiar: identities (e.g., 'I'm a teacher'), societal norms, logical thoughts, and physical routines. Its manifestations include:

- **Routine**: Morning coffee or work schedules, providing stability but risking stagnation (*Florentine Codex: Rituals*, Sahagún, 1950–1982).
- **Overthinking**: Analysing decisions (e.g., 'Should I take this job?'), imposing *Tlalticpac*'s order on uncertainty.

- **Fear of Change**: Clinging to roles during transitions (e.g., job loss), resisting *Teotl*'s flow.

Tlalticpac is essential—building relationships, societies, and meaning—but its rigidity traps *tonalli* (inner spark of *Teotl*). For example, believing 'I must succeed' limits fluidity, a challenge the *nahualli* addresses by questioning illusions (see Part 3, Chapter 17).

Teotl's Mystery in Daily Life

Teotl's Mystery breaks *Tlalticpac*'s grip, revealing *Teotl*'s boundless essence. It appears as:

- **Vivid Dreams**: Intense dreams bypassing logic, offering *Teotl's Mystery*'s truths (*Codex Borgia: Visions*, 1993).
- **Intuition**: Sudden insights (e.g., sensing a friend's need), defying rational explanation.
- **Synchronicity**: Uncanny coincidences (e.g., meeting someone with needed answers), hinting at *Teotl*'s weave.

These moments, guided by deities like *Tezcatlipoca* (see Part 3, Chapter 16), are doorways to transformation. A dream of a jaguar may spark courage, aligning *tonalli* with *Teotl*. The *nahualli* harnesses these through practises like shapeshifting (see Part 3, Chapter 18), balancing *Teotl's Mystery*'s chaos.

The Nahualli's Balance

The *nahualli* lives fluidly between worlds, using *Tlalticpac*'s stability to ground actions (e.g., teaching, parenting) and *Teotl's Mystery*'s fluidity to transform (e.g., dissolving ego). They model balance, as seen in *Florentine Codex* accounts of *nahualli* guiding communities. For example, a *nahualli* facing a conflict asks, 'What illusion holds me?' (see Part 3, Chapter 17), merging *Tlalticpac*'s clarity with *Teotl's Mystery*'s insight. This balance is accessible to all through *nahuallotl* practises (see Part 3, Chapter 19), preparing for the *Unknowable*'s vastness (see Chapter 13), which lies beyond even *Teotl's Mystery*.

Exercise 1: Dream Journaling

Explore *Teotl's Mystery* with this 15-minute nightly exercise:

1. **Prepare**: Place a notebook by your bed. Set an intention: 'I open to *Teotl's Mystery* through dreams.'

2. **Sleep**: Note any dream upon waking, even fragments (e.g., 'jaguar in a forest').

3. **Reflect**: Write the dream's feelings or symbols. Ask, 'What truth lies beyond *Tlalticpac*?'

4. **Ground**: If unsettled, sip water or touch earth to stabilise. **Urban Alternative**: Use a phone app for notes in a small apartment. **Safety**: Limit reflection to 15 minutes; pause if anxious, breathing deeply. This aligns with Part 3's dream-work (see Part 3, Chapter 15).

Exercise 2: Questioning Identity

Loosen *Tlalticpac*'s grip with this 10-minute exercise:

1. **Find a Space**: Sit quietly (e.g., park, room corner).

2. **Identify**: Note a *Tlalticpac* role (e.g., 'I'm a worker'). Journal it.

3. **Question**: Ask, 'Who is the 'I' in this role?' Feel *Teotl's Mystery*'s fluidity.

1. **Ground**: If uneasy, hold a stone or breathe slowly. **Urban Alternative**: Use a windowsill or headphones in a city. **Safety**: Limit to 10 minutes; stop if overwhelmed, grounding with water. This previews Part 3's guiding questions (see Part 3, Chapter 17).

Moving Forward

Living between *Tlalticpac* and *Teotl's Mystery* is *nahuallotl*'s heart, a mystical dance the *nahualli* embodies (see Part 3, Chapter 19). These exercises open *Teotl's Mystery*'s door, preparing for rituals (see Part 3, Chapter 18) and the *Unknowable*'s silent abyss (see Chapter 13), where even *Teotl* fades.

Thirteen

The Unknowable

Beyond the Edge of Existence

IN AZTEC COSMOLOGY, *TEOTL'S Mystery*—the realm of dreams, shapeshifting, and intuition—marks the boundary of what the *nahualli* can touch through *Teotl*'s flow (*Florentine Codex*). Yet beyond this lies the *Unknowable*, an abyss so absolute it defies mind, spirit, or even *Teotl* itself. Unlike *Teotl's Mystery*, which the *nahualli* navigates (see Chapter 12), the *Unknowable* is unreachable, a silent enigma that humbles all. This chapter explores the *Unknowable*, contrasting it with *Teotl's Mystery*, and offers a reflection to embrace its mystery, preparing for *nahuallotl*'s surrender (see Part 3, Chapter 15).

Teotl's Mystery vs. The Unknowable

Teotl's Mystery is the chaotic, transformative expanse where *Tlalticpac*'s illusions dissolve. Guided by deities like *Tezcatlipoca*, lord of transformation (*Codex Borgia*, 1993), the *nahualli* enters it through rituals (e.g., mirror-work, Part 3, Chapter 18) or dreams, merging *tonalli* with *Teotl*. A synchronicity or vision is a glimpse of *Teotl's Mystery*, accessible yet profound.

The *Unknowable*, however, lies beyond. It is not emptiness, nothingness, or even chaos—it transcends all concepts. No ritual, enlightenment, or death reaches it, as *Xolotl*, deity of liminality, guards thresholds *Teotl's Mystery* crosses but the *Unknowable* does not (Sahagún, 1950–1982).

Where *Teotl's Mystery* allows intuition, the *Unknowable* permits no knowing; where *Teotl's Mystery* transforms, the *Unknowable* leaves no trace. Imagine *Teotl's Mystery* as an ocean the *nahualli* swims; the *Unknowable* is the blackness beneath, where even water ceases.

The Unknowable in Nahuallotl

The *Unknowable* shapes *nahuallotl* not by pursuit but by surrender. It reminds the *nahualli* that even *Teotl's Mystery* is a veil, and true freedom lies in accepting limits. As *Tezcatlipoca* reveals illusions, the *Unknowable* silences ambition, fostering humility. The *nahualli* does not seek the *Unknowable* but honours it, living fluidly in *Tlalticpac* and *Teotl's Mystery* (see Chapter 15). This humility grounds *nahuallotl*, a mystical stance before *Teotl*'s infinite depths.

Reflection: Contemplating the Unknowable

Engage the *Unknowable*'s mystery with this 15-minute exercise:

1. **Prepare**: Find a quiet space (e.g., park, room). Hold an unanswerable question (e.g., 'What is beyond existence?').

2. **Contemplate**: Sit with the question, not seeking answers. Let thoughts dissolve, feeling the *Unknowable*'s vastness.

3. **Journal**: Write what arose—silence, awe, or unease. Note how it differs from *Teotl's Mystery*'s intuition.

4. **Ground**: If unsettled, touch earth or drink some water to stabilise. **Urban Alternative**: Gaze at stars from a rooftop or through a window, imagining a void beyond. **Safety**: Limit to 15 minutes; pause if anxious, breathing deeply. This reflection echoes *nahuallotl*'s surrender (see Part 3, Chapter 15).

Moving Forward

The *Unknowable* is *Teotl*'s silent core, humbling the *nahualli* as they weave *Tlalticpac* and *Teotl's Mystery*. Carry this awe into *nahuallotl* (Part 3), where surrender to *Teotl*'s mystery begins.

Interlude: From Movement to Guide

In *The Movement*, you learned to weave *Tlalticpac*'s edges with *Teotl's Mystery*'s flow. You danced between dualities—light and shadow, known and unknown—surrendering to the *Unknowable*'s embrace (*Codex Borgia*, 1993). Your *nahualli*'s qualities—perhaps a jaguar's stealth, a dog's loyalty—became threads in this tapestry, guiding you to live fluidly, neither bound nor adrift. This weaving is the *nahualli*'s art: to exist as *Teotl*'s breath, formless yet present.

Now, *Part 3: The Guide* calls you to embody this art for others. As a *nahualli*, you will become a threshold keeper, guiding seekers to dissolve their own illusions, freeing their *tonalli* to flow. The *Movement* prepared you to live *Teotl's Mystery*; the *Guide* empowers you to share it. Step forward with the fluidity you've woven, ready to hold space for others' unravelling.

Exercise: Preparing to Guide (10 minutes)

Sit in a quiet space, feet flat on the floor, hands resting open. Close your eyes and breathe deeply for 1 minute, feeling *Tlalticpac*'s stability beneath you. Envisage your *nahualli* beside you—its form, its energy. Ask silently, 'What quality do I offer as a guide?' (e.g., clarity, strength). Let its answer rise as a sensation, a word, an image. Hold this quality in your chest, imagining it as a light you'll share with others. Open your eyes, carrying this light into *Part 3*.

Part 3: The Guide

Fourteen

Introducing the Nahualli

The Nahualli in Aztec Context

IN AZTEC METAPHYSICS, A *nahualli* is a transformer who navigates *Teotl's Mystery*—the vast, unknowable flow of sacred energy (*teotl*)—to dissolve the illusions of *Tlalticpac*, the known world of forms and roles. Rooted in sources like the *Florentine Codex* and *Codex Borgia*, the *nahualli* is not a shaman in the modern sense, nor a figure from Castaneda's 'nagual' mythology. They are a conduit of transformation, guiding others to release attachments and align with the formless truth of *teotl*. This chapter introduces the *nahualli*'s role, core concepts, and the demanding path of *nahuallotl* (the way of the *nahualli*).

The Nahualli's Role: Beyond Healing

Unlike healers or priests who reinforce *Tlalticpac*'s structures (e.g., fixing bodies, soothing minds), a *nahualli* dismantles illusions to free the *tonalli*—the inner spark of *teotl* within each being. Their work is not comfort but truth, often unsettling as it strips away false identities.

What a Nahualli Does:

- Dissolves illusions, like roles ('I am a parent') or fears ('I am unworthy').
- Guides others to *Teotl's Mystery*, where self and world blur.

- Embodies *teotl*, acting as a bridge between *Tlalticpac* and the unknown.

- Challenges attachments, freeing *tonalli* to flow.

What a Nahualli Does Not Do:

- Heal or fix, as these preserve *Tlalticpac*'s illusions.

- Comfort or coddle, as truth requires facing discomfort.

- Seek power or control, as *teotl* is beyond possession.

- Reinforce the self, as *nahuallotl* is about dissolution.

For example, when someone says, 'I need healing from grief,' a *nahualli* might ask, 'Who is the 'I' that grieves?' Through questions or rituals, they guide the person to see grief as a fleeting form, not a fixed truth, freeing them to flow with *Teotl's Mystery*.

Teotl's Mystery vs. Tlalticpac: Core Concepts

The *nahualli*'s work hinges on two realms: *Teotl's Mystery* and *Tlalticpac*. Imagine *Tlalticpac* as a map of named places—jobs, roles, emotions—where everything is defined and separate. *Teotl's Mystery* is the uncharted wilderness beyond the map, where boundaries dissolve, and all is one flowing *teotl*. The *nahualli* navigates this wilderness, helping others release *Tlalticpac*'s grip.

Key concepts include:

- **Teotl**: The sacred energy permeating all existence, formless and dynamic (Sahagún, 1950–1982).

- **Tonalli**: The inner spark of *teotl* in each being, often trapped by *Tlalticpac*'s illusions.

- **Tlalticpac**: The known world of forms, where illusions like 'I am my job' take root.

- **Teotl's Mystery**: The unknown, where *teotl* flows without names or boundaries.

A *nahualli* does not add to *Tlalticpac*'s map but burns it away, revealing the wilderness of *Teotl's Mystery*. This contrasts with modern spiritualities, like New Age shamanism, which often reinforce the self (e.g., 'I am a healed soul') rather than dissolving it. As James Maffie notes in *Aztec Philosophy*, *teotl* is not a deity but a process, and the *nahualli* embodies this process, not a title.

The Nahualli Path: Surrender and Transformation

The path of *nahuallotl* is not for the faint-hearted. It demands surrender to *Teotl's Mystery*, where certainty and control vanish, and the *nahualli*—guided by their co-essence, the animal double (*nahualli*) tied to their *tonalli*—becomes like wind—formless, invisible, yet powerful—moving through *Tlalticpac* without being bound by it. This requires:

- **Releasing the self**: Letting go of identities, desires, and fears that anchor one to *Tlalticpac*.

- **Embracing chaos**: Accepting *Teotl's Mystery*'s unpredictability, where truth is fluid.

- **Courage**: Facing the discomfort of dissolution, as illusions crumble.

Unlike modern spiritual paths that promise growth or peace, *nahuallotl* offers no rewards, only alignment with *teotl*. The *nahualli* does not gain power but becomes a vessel, empty yet full of *Teotl's Mystery*. This path is solitary yet connected, as the *nahualli* serves others by guiding them to the same edge.

Reflection: Stepping Toward Teotl's Mystery

The *nahualli*'s journey begins with a single question: What illusions hold you in *Tlalticpac*? Reflect on a role (e.g., 'I am a worker'), fear (e.g., 'I am not enough'), or attachment (e.g., 'I need approval'). Write it down and ask, 'Who is the 'I' in this thought?' This simple act mirrors the *nahualli*'s work, loosening *Tlalticpac*'s grip. As we explore *nahuallotl* further, hold this question close, preparing to step toward *Teotl's Mystery*.

Fifteen

Becoming a Nahualli

Embodying Nahuallotl

To BECOME A NAHUALLI is to embody *nahuallotl*—the way of dissolving *Tlalticpac*'s illusions and aligning with *Teotl's Mystery*, the boundless flow of sacred energy (*teotl*). This chapter, grounded in the *Florentine Codex* and *Codex Borgia*, explores the practises and mindset that transform a practitioner into a vessel for *teotl*. Unlike modern spiritual paths that seek control or growth, *nahuallotl* demands surrender, fluidity, and courage. Through practises like dream-work and shapeshifting, and a mindset of letting go, the *nahualli* becomes a bridge between the known (*Tlalticpac*) and the unknown (*Teotl's Mystery*), living *teotl* in every moment.

Practises: Dream Work, Shapeshifting, Breaking Rules

A *nahualli* practises lucid dreaming to explore *Teotl's Mystery*'s layers, asking in dreams, 'What is formless?' Answers arrive as symbols—a jaguar's shadow, a river's song—revealing truths beyond *Tlalticpac*'s veil.

A *nahualli*—the guide who walks the path of *nahuallotl*—embodies their co-essence, the animal double (*nahualli*) destined at birth, such as a jaguar or dog, to transcend human limits. In *nahuallotl*, this co-essence is your spiritual counterpart, tied to your *tonalli* and revealed through *Teotl*'s design (*Florentine Codex: Book 11*, Sahagún, 1950–1982), reflecting qualities like a jaguar's courage or a dog's loyalty.

- **Dream-Work**: In dreams, *Tlalticpac*'s rules soften, offering glimpses of *Teotl's Mystery*. A *nahualli* practises lucid dreaming to navigate this realm consciously, meeting co-essences (animal or spirit forms of *tonalli*) or dissolving illusions (e.g., a dream role like 'I am a failure'). Start by journaling dreams nightly, noting recurring symbols. If overwhelmed, ground yourself post-dream by touching earth or drinking water to reconnect with *Tlalticpac*.

- **Shapeshifting**: A *nahualli*—the guide who walks the path of *nahuallotl*—embodies their co-essence, the animal double (*nahualli*) destined at birth, such as a jaguar or dog, to transcend human limits. In *nahuallotl*, this co-essence is your spiritual counterpart, tied to your *tonalli* and revealed through *Teotl's* design (*Florentine Codex: Book 11*, Sahagún, 1950–1982), reflecting qualities like a jaguar's courage or an eagle's vision. This embodiment is not physical but energetic, a merging with your co-essence's essence to awaken its power within. Detailed rituals are in Chapter 18, but begin by meditating on your co-essence—your destined *nahualli* or an animal you feel drawn to if its form is yet unknown. Imagine its movement in your body, letting its spirit flow through your limbs as *Teotl's* breath.

- **Deepening Your *Nahualli* Connection:** Having identified your *nahualli* in the *Introduction*'s ritual, deepen this bond through dream work, a practice rooted in Aztec tradition where dreams reveal *Teotl's* truths (*Florentine Codex: Book 10*, Sahagún, 1950–1982). Before bed, place a token of your *nahualli* (e.g., a feather for an eagle, a stone for a jaguar; **urban alternative:** a key for a dog's loyalty) by your bedside, sit quietly, and recall its qualities (e.g., 'Dog: loyalty'). Speak softly, '*Nahualli*, walk with me in dreams. Share your wisdom,' visualising its form as you drift to sleep. Upon waking, write any dreams or sensations (e.g., 'Felt wings; heard a howl'), noting how its qualities appeared (e.g., 'Clarity in a decision'). Thank your *nahualli* silently, keeping the token near. If unsettled, sip water or touch the floor. Repeat over

- **Breaking Tlalticpac's Rules**: *Tlalticpac* binds through routines and roles. A *nahualli* disrupts these subtly—eating with the opposite hand, walking backwards under moonlight, or questioning thoughts like 'I must succeed.' These acts, described in *Codex Borgia*, loosen *Tlalticpac*'s hold, fostering fluidity.

Safety is key: if practises feel destabilising, pause and focus on grounding (e.g., deep breathing, physical touch). These practises build the *nahualli*'s ability to flow, not to conquer.

Mindset: Surrender and Fluidity

Beyond practises, *nahuallotl* requires a mindset of surrender. As James Maffie notes in *Aztec Philosophy*, *teotl* is a process, not a possession. A *nahualli* does not control *Teotl's Mystery* but becomes its vessel, like a riverbed for water. This means:

- **Releasing the Self**: Letting go of identities (e.g., 'I am my job') and desires (e.g., 'I need approval'). When retrieving a 'lost soul,' a *nahualli* dissolves the illusion of separation, not restoring a fixed self, but freeing *tonalli* to flow.

- **Embracing Fluidity**: Accepting *Teotl's Mystery*'s chaos, where truth shifts like wind. A *nahualli* moves between *Tlalticpac* and the unknown, neither bound nor lost.

- **Becoming a Bridge**: By embodying *teotl*, the *nahualli* connects others to *Teotl's Mystery*, guiding without attachment.

For example, aligning with *Tezcatlipoca*'s transformative energy or *Xolotl*'s shadowy transitions (see Chapter 16) helps a *nahualli* surrender. This mindset is not achieved but lived, moment by moment.

Daily Life: Living Teotl's Mystery

Nahuallotl is not confined to rituals but shapes daily life. A *nahualli* weaves *Teotl's Mystery* into mundane moments, transforming how they move through *Tlalticpac*. For instance, during a stressful meeting, a *nahualli* might embody their jaguar co-essence—the animal double (*nahualli*) destined at birth—channelling its calm confidence to speak without attachment to outcomes. This fluidity affects relationships, work, and self-perception, as the *nahualli* sees all as *teotl*'s dance.

A simple daily practice can anchor this:

- **Morning Meditation (5 minutes)**: Sit quietly, feeling your breath as *teotl*'s flow. Sense *Teotl's Mystery* in your surroundings—wind, traffic, silence. Ask, 'What illusions can I release today?' Journal one insight (e.g., 'I don't need to please everyone'). If urban, use a windowsill to sit next to or a park to connect.

This practice, repeatable in any setting, builds the *nahualli*'s awareness of *teotl*. Over time, it reshapes *Tlalticpac*'s hold, making fluidity second nature.

Prompt: Sensing Teotl's Mystery

To begin embodying *nahuallotl*, try the morning meditation today. Spend 5 minutes sensing *Teotl's Mystery* in your environment—perhaps the breeze, a shadow, or your heartbeat. Journal one illusion (e.g., a role, fear) you might release. As we move to explore deities in *nahuallotl*, carry this awareness, preparing to align with *teotl*'s forces.

Sixteen

Deities in Nahuallotl

Deities as Forces of Teotl's Mystery

IN AZTEC METAPHYSICS, DEITIES like *Tezcatlipoca* and *Quetzalcoatl* are not gods to worship but dynamic forces of *Teotl's Mystery*—the formless flow of sacred energy (*teotl*). As described in the *Florentine Codex* and *Codex Borgia*, these forces embody aspects of *teotl*, guiding *nahualli* in dissolving *Tlalticpac*'s illusions. This chapter explores how *nahualli* engage deities through rituals and offerings, their unique roles in *nahuallotl*, and how to balance their energies. By aligning with these forces, a *nahualli* deepens their connection to *Teotl's Mystery*, navigating transformation, death, and creation.

Engaging Deities and Spirits: Rituals and Offerings

Nahualli connect with deities and spirits (e.g., ancestors, co-essences—the animal doubles (*nahualli*) tied to their *tonalli*) through simple, intentional practises, viewing them as expressions of *teotl*:

- **Offerings**: Present copal, maize, or flowers on a small altar (a windowsill works in urban settings). Speak your intention, e.g., 'I offer this to *Tezcatlipoca* for clarity.' Dispose of offerings respectfully, returning them to earth.

- **Scrying**: Use an obsidian mirror or dark water to glimpse *Teotl's Mystery* through a deity's lens (see Chapter 18 for mirror-work). Focus on a question, like 'What illusion must I release?'

- **Invocation**: Chant or speak the specific deity's name you are working with in a quiet space, inviting their energy. For example, call *Xolotl* during transitions, feeling their shadowy guidance. Be mindful of what you are invoking, as some deities are extremely powerful and unpredictable. The author recommends to not invoke any deity or spirit outside the scope of this book.

- **Spirit Work**: Spirit Work: Honour spirits (e.g., ancestors) with offerings or dream invitations, asking for wisdom. You might also connect with your co-essence, such as a jaguar or dog, by inviting its presence in dreams to reveal *Teotl's* guidance. Ground afterwards with water or touch to stay balanced.

Safety is vital: limit sessions to 20–30 minutes and ground if feeling unmoored (e.g., deep breathing). These practises, rooted in *Codex Borgia*, align *nahualli* with *teotl's* flow.

Deity Roles: Tezcatlipoca to Chalchiuhtlicue

Each deity offers unique guidance for *nahuallotl*. Below are key deities, their roles, and a brief ritual to engage them, adapted for accessibility.

- **Tezcatlipoca**: The Smoking Mirror embodies transformation and illusion-breaking. *Nahualli* invoke *Tezcatlipoca* to dissolve false identities (e.g., 'I am my failures'). **Ritual:** Light a candle before a dark surface (e.g., phone screen off). Gaze into it, asking, 'What illusion binds me?' Journal insights (10 minutes).

- **Mictlantecuhtli**: Lord of Mictlan, oversees the transitions of the dead, aiding *nahualli* in releasing attachments to loss. ***Ritual:*** Place a skull image on an altar, offer maize, and meditate on letting go of a past role to achieve release of loss, invoking Mictlantecuhtli's wisdom (15 minutes).

- **Quetzalcoatl**: The Feathered Serpent fosters wisdom and creativity. *Nahualli* seek *Quetzalcoatl* for insight in teaching or creating. ***Ritual:*** Draw a serpent, burn copal, and visualise a project's flow, noting inspired ideas (10 minutes).

- **Tlaloc**: The Rain Bringer purifies and renews. *Nahualli* invoke *Tlaloc* to cleanse emotional burdens. ***Ritual:*** Pour water into a bowl, speak a burden (e.g., 'I release guilt'), and pour it out, feeling renewal (10 minutes).

- **Xolotl**: The canine psychopomp, guides the *Nahualli* to embody *Teotl's* Mystery—not as a realm, but as the chaotic flow of *teotl* where *Tlaltipac's* illusions dissolve, as my 4 Dog *nahualli* has shown. ***Ritual:*** At dusk, walk slowly, offering tobacco, and ask *Xolotl* to guide a transition (15 minutes).

- **Chalchiuhtlicue**: The Jade Skirt governs waters and flow. *Nahualli* call *Chalchiuhtlicue* for emotional balance. ***Ritual:*** Hold a jade stone (or green object), dip fingers in water, and meditate on emotional flow (10 minutes).

These rituals, drawn from *Florentine Codex*, are starting points, deepened in Chapter 18.

Balancing Multiple Deities

A *nahualli* may work with multiple deities, choosing based on need or intuition. For example, *Tezcatlipoca* aids ego dissolution, while *Quetzalcoatl* sparks insight. To balance:

- **Listen Intuitively**: Notice which deity's energy (e.g., *Tlaloc*'s calm) feels relevant. Dreams or omens (e.g., rain) may guide.

- **Rotate Focus**: Dedicate days or weeks to one deity, avoiding overwhelm.

- **Unify in Teotl**: All deities are *teotl*'s facets. Offerings to one honour all, grounding the *nahualli* in *Teotl's Mystery*.

If energies feel intense, pause and ground with earth (e.g., barefoot walking). This balance, rooted in *Aztec Philosophy*, ensures *nahuallotl* remains fluid.

Table: Deity Associations

Deity	Role in Nahuallotl	Symbols	Ritual Offering	Ritual Focus
Tezcatlipoca	Transformation, Illusion-Breaking	Obsidian, Jaguar	Copal, Candle	Mirror Work
Mictlantecuhtli	Ruler of the Dead, Facilitator of Release	Skull	Maize	Release of Loss
Quetzalcoatl	Wisdom, Creativity	Serpent, Feathers	Copal, Paper	Creative Offering
Tlaloc	Purification, Renewal	Rain, Lightning	Water, Flowers	Elemental Connection
Xolotl	Psychopomp, Transitions, Duality	Dog, Twilight	Tobacco	Shapeshifting Embodiment
Chalchiuhtlicue	Emotional Balance, Flow	Jade, Rivers	Water, Jade	Elemental Connection

Reflection: Connecting with Deities

Which deity resonates with your current journey? Try their ritual (e.g., *Tlaloc*'s water pour for renewal) this week, noting how their energy shifts your awareness. As we explore guiding others in *nahuallotl*, carry this connection, aligning with *teotl*'s forces.

Seventeen

Guiding Transformation
The Nahualli as Threshold Keeper

Ethical Guidance: Responsibility in *Nahuallotl*

GUIDING AS A *NAHUALLI* carries deep responsibility. Ethical considerations ensure transformation respects the individual's journey:
Consent: Always seek permission before guiding, ensuring readiness (e.g., 'Are you open to questioning this belief?').
Boundaries: Respect limits, pausing if someone feels overwhelmed. Suggest grounding (e.g., touching earth) to stabilise.
Non-Attachment: Avoid imposing outcomes. A *nahualli* guides to *Teotl's Mystery*, not to their own vision.
Cultural Respect: Honor Aztec roots (Sahagún, 1950–1982), avoiding appropriation or modern distortions.

To assess readiness, *nahualli* observe signs of attachment (e.g., rigid self-descriptions like 'I am a failure') versus openness (e.g., curiosity about illusions). If unready, they suggest simpler practises (e.g., see Chapter 15's meditation) before rituals.

Cultural Ethics: Honouring Indigenous Roots

As a *nahualli*, you walk a path rooted in Aztec metaphysics, a living tradition that endures through Indigenous communities (Sahagún,

1950–1982). For non-Indigenous practitioners, this journey demands humility—*nahuallotl* is not a tool to claim but a sacred practice to respect. Engage ethically by learning from Indigenous voices, such as contemporary Nahua elders or scholars, and by honouring the cultural context of these teachings. Avoid appropriation by centring *Teotl*'s flow over personal gain, ensuring your practice uplifts the tradition's spirit rather than exploits it.

Case Study: A Nahualli at Work

Consider Maria, a teacher who says, 'I'm failing my students; I need to be better.' A *nahualli* notices her attachment to the role 'I am a teacher.' Drawing on the clarity of his dog co-essence, he asks, 'Who is the 'I' that fails?' Over tea, he guides Maria to journal this question, revealing her identity as a construct. In a ritual (see Chapter 18's mirror-work), Maria gazes into a dark surface, seeing her 'failure' as a fleeting image, not truth. After a week, she reports feeling lighter, teaching with less pressure, her *tonalli* freer to flow. The *nahualli* offered no comfort, only a path to *Teotl's Mystery*.

Handling Resistance in Guiding

Not all seekers will surrender easily to *Teotl's Mystery*. Resistance often arises when illusions—like 'I must be perfect'—are deeply rooted, binding the *tonalli* to *Tlalticpac*'s constructs (*Florentine Codex: Book 10*, Sahagún, 1950–1982). A *nahualli* meets resistance not with force but with presence, reflecting the seeker's words like a mirror, inviting them to see without judgment.

Consider Javier, who declares, 'I can't let go of my anger—it's who I am.' The *nahualli*, embodying her eagle *nahualli*'s clarity, responds, 'Who is the 'I' that holds anger?' Javier bristles, 'You don't understand—I need it to protect me!' Instead of debating, the *nahualli* sits in silence, offering space for Javier's words to echo. He then asks, 'What does anger protect?' This gentle probe, rooted in non-attachment (see 'Ethics: Guiding with

Care'), shifts Javier's gaze inward. Over time, he journals this question, uncovering that anger shields a fear of vulnerability—a construct, not truth. The *nahualli*'s role is not to fix but to hold space, trusting *Teotl*'s flow to unravel illusions at its own pace.

Prompt: Questioning the Self

To practice guiding, ask yourself, 'Who is the 'I' in my current challenge?' (e.g., 'I am stressed'). Write the thought and question it: 'What is this 'I' separate from?' Spend 5 minutes reflecting, noting shifts in perception. As we move to *nahuallotl* rituals, carry this question, preparing to guide or be guided.

Eighteen

Rituals of Nahuallotl

Rituals as Nahuallotl Practice

RITUALS ARE DOORWAYS TO *Teotl's Mystery*, the boundless flow of sacred energy (*teotl*), allowing *nahualli* and practitioners to dissolve *Tlalticpac*'s illusions and align with *teotl*. Rooted in the *Florentine Codex* and *Codex Borgia*, these five rituals—obsidian mirror-work, shapeshifting embodiment, psychopomp journey, elemental connection, and offering to spirits—are accessible to all with courage. Each includes urban alternatives and safety tips, ensuring practicality. Begin by preparing a sacred space: clear a quiet area (e.g., a corner, balcony), set an intention (e.g., 'I release illusions'), and ground with deep breathing. If overwhelmed, pause and touch earth or drink water. This chapter, grounded in *Aztec Philosophy*, equips you to practice *nahuallotl*.

Table: Ritual Overview

Ritual	Purpose	Materials	Frequency	Urban Alternative
Obsidian Mirror-Work	Dissolve ego/illusions with Tezcatlipoca	Obsidian mirror, candle, journal	Weekly	Phone screen (off), bowl of water
Psychopomp Journey	Guide souls, release loss (Xolotl/Mictlantecuhtli)	Skull image, maize, blanket	As needed	Printed skull, rice, shawl or cloth
Serpent's Creative Offering	Channel wisdom/creativity with Quetzalcoatl	Copal, paper, feathers, journal	Weekly	Incense sticks, notebook paper, craft feathers
Rain's Elemental Connection	Purify/renew with Tlaloc	Water, flowers, lightning imagery, bowl	Monthly	Bottled water, dried flowers, storm playlist
Xolotl Shapeshifting Embodiment	Embody co-essence with Xolotl	Feathers, music, space to move, tobacco	Biweekly	Headphones, small room, tobacco on windowsill
Jade River Flow	Balance emotions with Chalchiuhtlicue	Water, jade, journal	Weekly	Tap water, green glass piece

Ritual 1: Obsidian Mirror-Work

Purpose: Dissolve ego and illusions (e.g., 'I am my role') by confronting Tlalticpac's reflections, aligning with Tezcatlipoca's transformative energy (Sahagún, 1950–1982). **Materials:** Obsidian mirror (or dark phone screen/bowl of water), candle, journal. **Steps** (20 minutes):

1. Set a sacred space at night. Light a candle, place the mirror before you.

2. State your intention: 'I seek to release illusions with Tezcatlipoca.'

3. Gaze into the mirror, asking, 'Who is the 'I' I cling to?' (e.g., 'I am a worker').

4. Observe images or feelings without judgement. Let them fade, feeling teotl's flow.

5. Journal insights (e.g., 'My role is not me'). Extinguish the candle. **Urban Alternative:** Use a phone screen (off) or a bowl of water in a quiet room. **Safety:** If unsettled, ground by touching earth or sip some water. Limit to 20 minutes. **Frequency:** Weekly, reflecting on one illusion per session.

Ritual 2: Xolotl Shapeshifting Embodiment

Purpose: Embody a co-essence—the animal double (nahualli) destined at birth, such as a jaguar or dog—to transcend Tlalticpac's limits, fostering fluidity with Xolotl's guidance (*Codex Borgia*, 1993). **Materials:** Feathers (or paper), music (drums or playlist), space to move, tobacco. **Steps** (15 minutes):

1. Prepare a space (indoor/outdoor) at dusk, offering tobacco to honour Xolotl.

2. Play music, hold feathers, setting the intention: 'I embody my co-essence with Xolotl's aid.'

3. Meditate on an animal (e.g., dog, reflecting Xolotl's form), visualising its traits (e.g., loyalty, instinct).

4. Move as the animal—walk, sway, or mimic its motions—feeling its energy in your body.

5. Return slowly, journaling how the co-essence shifts your perspective, and close by thanking Xolotl. Urban Alternative: Use headphones and a small room, moving gently; offer tobacco in a small bowl, placing it on a windowsill afterwards. **Safety:** Stop if dizzy; ground with deep breaths. Avoid overexertion. **Frequency:** Biweekly, exploring one co-essence per session.

Ritual 3: Psychopomp Journey

Purpose: Guide souls through Mictlan (with Xolotl's guidance) and release loss (under Mictlantecuhtli's oversight) to facilitate transitions (*Florentine Codex: Book 3*, Sahagún, 1950–1982). **Materials:** Skull image, maize, blanket. Steps (30 minutes):

1. Create a dark, quiet space. Place the skull and maize on an altar.

2. Set intention: 'I call on Xolotl to guide [name/soul] through Mictlan, and Mictlantecuhtli to release [name/loss].'

3. Lie under the blanket, visualise a journey (avoid narrating as much as possible) a journey to Mictlan (a dark, calm realm).

4. Meet the soul/loss, asking, 'What holds you?' With Xolotl's guidance, offer maize, helping them flow through Mictlan.

5. Return, journal insights, and scatter maize outside (or dispose respectfully). Urban Alternative: Use a printed skull image (e.g., from an Aztec codex, found online) or a

6. digital display on a phone to invoke Mictlantecuhtli, rice in a small bowl as the offering, and a shawl or cloth in place of a blanket. Visualise indoors, and place the rice

7. bowl on a windowsill for a day before discarding respectfully. **Safety:** If heavy emotions arise, pause and ground with water. Limit to 30 minutes. **Frequency:** As needed, for specific transitions or losses.

Ritual 4: Serpent's Creative Offering

Purpose: Channel wisdom and creativity for inspiration, invoking Quetzalcoatl's serpentine energy to guide projects or ideas (*Florentine Codex: Book 1*, Sahagún, 1950–1982). **Materials:** Copal, paper, feathers, journal. Steps (15 minutes):

1. Set a sacred space during the day. Burn copal, place paper and feathers before you.

2. State your intention: 'I seek Quetzalcoatl's wisdom to inspire my [project/idea].'

3. Draw a serpent on the paper, visualising the project's flow and potential.

4. Hold the feathers, feeling creative energy rise, and note any inspired ideas.

5. Journal insights (e.g., 'A new perspective emerged'). Offer the paper by burning or keeping it respectfully. **Urban Alternative:** Use incense sticks, notebook paper, and craft feathers in a well-lit room. **Safety:** If overwhelmed, pause and breathe deeply. Limit to 15 minutes. **Frequency:** Weekly, to sustain creative flow.

Ritual 5: Rain's Elemental Connection

Purpose: Purify and renew through connection with water elements, invoking Tlaloc's cleansing rain to release burdens (*Florentine Codex: Book 1*, Sahagún, 1950–1982). **Materials:** Water, flowers, lightning imagery (e.g., a drawn symbol), bowl. **Steps** (20 minutes):

1. Set a sacred space, ideally outdoors during rain. Place water and flowers in a bowl.

2. State your intention: 'I seek Tlaloc's renewal to release [burden, e.g., guilt].'

3. Hold the lightning imagery, visualising rain washing away the burden.

4. Pour the water over the flowers, feeling purification and renewal in your body.

5. Journal the experience (e.g., 'I feel lighter'). Dispose of the water

and flowers respectfully outside. **Urban Alternative:** Use bottled water, dried flowers, and a storm sound playlist in a quiet room. **Safety:** If emotions surge, pause and sip water to ground. Limit to 20 minutes. **Frequency:** Monthly, during rain or storms if possible.

Ritual 6: Jade River Flow

Purpose: Balance emotions and foster flow through connection with water, invoking Chalchiuhtlicue's nurturing rivers (*Florentine Codex: Book 1*, Sahagún, 1950–1982). **Materials:** Water, jade (or green stone), journal. **Steps** (15 minutes):

Set a sacred space near water if possible. Hold the jade, place water in a bowl.

State your intention: 'I seek Chalchiuhtlicue's flow to balance [emotion, e.g., anger].'

Dip your fingers in the water, visualising a river carrying away the emotion.

Feel the jade's energy, letting emotional balance settle in your body.

Journal the experience (e.g., 'I feel calmer'). Pour the water outside respectfully. **Urban Alternative:** Use tap water and a green glass piece in a quiet room. **Safety**: If emotions overwhelm, pause and breathe deeply. Limit to 15 minutes. **Frequency:** Weekly, to maintain emotional balance.

Reflection: Choosing a Ritual

Which ritual calls to you—dissolving an illusion, embodying a co-essence, or honouring a spirit? Try one this week, noting how it shifts your connection to *Teotl's Mystery*. As we conclude with living as a *nahualli*, carry these practises, weaving *nahuallotl* into your life.

Nineteen

Living as a Nahualli

The Nahualli Journey

LIVING AS A NAHUALLI means weaving *Teotl's Mystery*—the boundless flow of sacred energy (*teotl*)—into every moment, dissolving *Tlalticpac*'s illusions to embody *nahuallotl*. Rooted in the *Florentine Codex* and *Codex Borgia*, this journey transforms not just the practitioner but their world. This final chapter revisits core practises, explores how *nahualli* apply *Teotl's Mystery* in daily life, and considers their impact on community. It concludes with a practical exercise to begin living *nahuallotl*, grounding the path in *Aztec Philosophy*'s vision of *teotl* as a dynamic process.

Core Practises Revisited

The *nahualli*'s path rests on practises that loosen *Tlalticpac*'s grip, detailed in Chapters 15 and 18:

- **Dream-Work**: Navigating dreams to meet co-essences or dissolve illusions (e.g., 'I am unworthy') prepares *nahualli* to flow in *Teotl's Mystery*. Journaling dreams nightly builds this skill (see Chapter 15).

- **Shapeshifting**: Embodying a co-essence—the animal double (*nahualli*) destined at birth—(e.g., jaguar's courage) transcends human limits, fostering fluidity. Rituals in Chapter 18 guide this practice, adaptable to urban spaces.

- **Death as Transition**: Viewing death (literal or metaphorical) as a shift to *Teotl's Mystery* frees *tonalli*. Psychopomp rituals (see Chapter 18) train *nahualli* to guide such transitions.

Initiation rites like fasting or isolation, described in *Codex Borgia*, mark commitment to *nahuallotl*. These may be brief (e.g., a day of silence) or intense (e.g., a night alone), but all reinforce surrender to *teotl*. Urban practitioners can adapt by using quiet rooms or parks.

Daily Life: Applying Teotl's Mystery

Nahuallotl transforms daily life, as *nahualli* live between *Tlalticpac* and *Teotl's Mystery*. For example:

- **Parenting**: A *nahualli* parent, facing a child's tantrum, breathes *teotl*'s flow, responding without attachment to 'I must control.' They ask, 'What is this moment teaching?' fostering calm.

- **Work**: In a tense meeting, a *nahualli* channels their dog co-essence's clarity—the animal double (*nahualli*) tied to their *tonalli*—speaking truth without fear of judgement, seeing colleagues as *teotl*'s expressions.

- **Self-Perception**: When doubt arises ('I'm not enough'), a *nahualli* questions, 'Who is the 'I'?' dissolving the thought, aligning with *Teotl's Mystery*.

These moments, small yet profound, make *nahuallotl* a lived reality. A daily meditation (see Chapter 15) sustains this, grounding *nahualli* in *teotl*'s presence amid *Tlalticpac*.

Community Impact: Inspiring Transformation

Nahualli ripple beyond themselves, inspiring communities to question *Tlalticpac*'s illusions. By embodying *teotl*—fluid, unattached, truthful—they model a way of being that challenges rigid roles (e.g., 'I am my job'). A *nahualli* teaching a ritual (see Chapter 18) might guide neighbours to release fears, fostering collective openness. In markets or gatherings, their presence—calm yet intense—prompts others to pause, sense *teotl*, and reconsider their stories. As *Florentine Codex* suggests, *nahualli* transform consciousness not by preaching but by being, aligning communities with *Teotl's Mystery*.

Call to Action: A Nahuallotl Plan

Living as a *nahualli* requires sustained practice, a weaving of *Teotl's Mystery* into each moment. This 28-day plan guides you through four weeks of *nah'uallotl*, building from personal transformation to community impact. Each week deepens your path, drawing on practises from this book.

Week 1: Shedding Illusions

Focus on dissolving *Tlalticpac*'s illusions, grounding your *tonalli*.

- **Day 1**: Journal a daily illusion (e.g., 'I am my job'). Reflect: 'What binds me to this?'

- **Day 2**: Practice mirror-work (see Chapter 18) to see the illusion as a construct, gazing for 5 minutes.

- **Day 3**: Break a *Tlalticpac* rule (see Chapter 15), like eating with the opposite hand, to foster fluidity.

- **Day 4**: Revisit the *Introduction*'s ritual (see Introduction) to reconnect with your *nahualli*, noting any new insights.

- **Day 5**: Journal: 'What illusion feels lighter?' Burn or bury the paper as a release, honouring *Teotl*'s flow.

- **Day 6**: Walk in nature (or a park) for 15 minutes, observing *Tlalticpac*'s forms without naming them (e.g., 'tree' becomes 'shape').

- **Day 7**: Reflect: 'What shifted this week?' Drink water, grounding your *tonalli*.

Week 2: Deepening Your *Nahualli* Connection

Strengthen your bond with your *nahualli*, embodying its essence.

- **Day 8**: Practice the 'Deepening Your *Nahualli* Connection' ritual (see Chapter 15), inviting your *nahualli* in dreams.
- **Day 9**: Embody your *nahualli* (see Chapter 18's Shapeshifting Embodiment), moving as the animal for 10 minutes. Journal its qualities.
- **Day 10**: In a quiet moment, ask your *nahualli*, 'What do I need today?' Listen for a sensation or image (e.g., 'calm,' 'strength').
- **Day 11**: Create a small token for your *nahualli* (e.g., draw a jaguar, fold an origami eagle). Place it where you'll see it daily.
- **Day 12**: Practice lucid dreaming (see Chapter 15), asking, 'What is my *nahualli*'s message?' Record the dream.
- **Day 13**: Channel your *nahualli*'s quality in a daily task (e.g., eagle's clarity in a decision). Note how it shifts your approach.
- **Day 14**: Reflect: 'How has my *nahualli* guided me?' Thank it silently, feeling *Teotl*'s presence.

Week 3: Guiding Others

Apply your practice to guide others, holding space for their unravelling.

- **Day 15**: Ask a friend, 'What do you cling to?' Listen without advising, journaling their response.
- **Day 16**: Practice mirror-work with a partner (see Chapter 18), guiding them to see an illusion (e.g., 'I must be perfect').

- **Day 17**: If resistance arises, use the approach from Chapter 17 (Handling Resistance in Guiding): ask, 'What does [illusion] protect?' Hold space for their answer.

- **Day 18**: Make an offering to a spirit or deity (see Chapter 18) for guidance in your role as a *nahualli*.

- **Day 19**: Journal: 'What did I learn from guiding?' Notice your attachments (e.g., 'I must help').

- **Day 20**: Share a *nahuallotl* insight with someone (e.g., 'Illusions bind us, but we can release them'). Observe their reaction.

- **Day 21**: Reflect: 'How did I embody the *nahualli*'s role?' Ground by touching earth or sipping water.

Week 4: Weaving Community

Integrate *nahuallotl* into your community, becoming *Teotl*'s breath.

- **Day 22**: Perform a small, unseen-act of kindness in your community (e.g., leave a note of encouragement), echoing the exercise 'The Weightless Act' (see Chapter 1).

- **Day 23**: Host a small gathering (or virtual call) to share a *nahuallotl* practice, like a group dream-reflection (see Chapter 15).

- **Day 24**: Embody your *nahualli* in a community setting (e.g., dog's courage in a meeting). Note its impact.

- **Day 25**: Make a collective offering (see Chapter 18) with others, honouring a shared spirit or ancestor.

- **Day 26**: Journal: 'How does *Teotl's Mystery* flow through my community?' Look for patterns of connection.

- **Day 27**: Break a collective *Tlalticpac* rule (e.g., turn off devices for an hour together), fostering fluidity as a group.

- **Day 28**: Reflect: 'What shifted this month?' Share your journey with a trusted friend or community, celebrating *Teotl*'s dance.

Acknowledgements

This guidebook owes its depth and authenticity to the rich legacy of Aztec wisdom preserved through ancient manuscripts and the dedicated work of scholars who have illuminated their meanings. I am profoundly grateful to the creators of the *Florentine Codex*, *Codex Borgia*, *Codex Borbonicus*, *Codex Magliabechiano*, *Codex Mendoza*, and *Codex Vaticanus A*, whose records of rituals, cosmology, and *nahuallotl* practises form the foundation of this work. Institutions such as Fondo de Cultura Económica, Dover Publications, University of California Press, and Akademische Druck- und Verlagsanstalt have ensured these codices remain accessible, and their efforts are deeply appreciated.

Special thanks are due to contemporary scholars whose research has guided this exploration of Aztec metaphysics. James Maffie's *Aztec Philosophy: Understanding a World in Motion* provided an invaluable framework for understanding *teotl*, *tonalli*, and *Tlalticpac*. The works of Manuel Aguilar-Moreno, Elizabeth Hill Boone, and Davíd Carrasco offered critical insights into Aztec rituals and cosmology, enriching the cultural context of this guidebook.

Above all, I honour the enduring spirit of the Aztec people, whose profound connection to *Teotl's Mystery* inspires these pages. This work is a humble attempt to share their wisdom with modern seekers, fostering transformation through the path of the *nahualli*. To all who have preserved and shared this knowledge, past and present, my heartfelt gratitude.

Appendix A

The 20 Day Signs of the Tonalpohualli

This list presents the 20 sacred day signs of the Aztec Tonalpohualli calendar in their traditional order, along with a simple, core meaning for each.

1. **Cipactli (Crocodile):** Primal earth energy, beginnings, nourishment, and survival.

2. **Ehecatl (Wind):** Communication, spirit, intelligence, and the unseen forces of life.

3. **Calli (House):** Stability, family, protection, and the body as a home for the spirit.

4. **Cuetzpalin (Lizard):** Abundance, agility, regeneration, and sexual potency.

5. **Coatl (Serpent):** Life force, transformation, shedding the old, and primal energy.

6. **Miquiztli (Death):** Endings, cosmic transformation, letting go, and honoring ancestors.

7. **Mazatl (Deer):** Grace, intuition, alertness, tracking, and the spirit of the hunt.

8. **Tochtli (Rabbit):** Fertility, abundance, self-sacrifice, and the energy of the moon.

9. **Atl (Water):** Emotion, purification, cleansing, and the flow of life.

10. **Itzcuintli (Dog):** Loyalty, guidance through darkness, and companionship on the soul's journey.

11. **Ozomatli (Monkey):** Artistry, pleasure, celebration, chaos, and spontaneity.

12. **Malinalli (Grass):** Healing, regeneration, community, and overcoming obstacles with tenacity.

13. **Acatl (Reed):** Authority, spiritual warfare, ancestral wisdom, and righteous action.

14. **Jaguar (Ocelot/Jaguar):** Shamanic, night vision, hidden power, and the heart of the mountain.

15. **Cuauhtli (Eagle):** Vision, courage, solar power, the spirit of the warrior.

16. **Cozcacuauhtli (Vulture):** Purification, cleansing of karma, long life, and wisdom.

17. **Olin (Movement/Earthquake):** Transformation, change, fate, and the rhythm of the cosmos.

18. **Tecpatl (Flint/Knife):** Truth, sacrifice, trial, clarity, and the sharp edge of reality.

19. **Quiahuitl (Rain):** Cleansing storms, reliance on fate, emotional release, and divine grace.

20. **Xochitl (Flower):** Beauty, love, art, poignancy, and the fleeting nature of life.

Appendix B

Contextualising the Nahualli Path in Mesoamerica

While this handbook is dedicated to the specific path of the Aztec *nahualli*, the reader may find it helpful to understand this tradition within the broader context of Mesoamerican thought. The great civilisations of Mesoamerica, including the Olmec, Maya, Toltec, and Aztec, were not isolated. They engaged in centuries of trade, warfare, and cultural exchange, resulting in a shared cosmological foundation, even as each culture developed its own unique expression of it.

Mesoamerican cultures broadly shared a world-view organised by cyclical time, a complex pantheon of deities representing natural forces, and a profound connection between human destiny and the cosmos. However, the languages, specific deities, and ritual practices often differed significantly.

The Toltec Heritage

The Aztecs revered the Toltecs, who preceded them as legendary masters of art, wisdom, and architecture. This reverence has been adopted by some modern spiritual authors who claim a "Toltec nagual lineage". As stated in the preface of this work, such claims lack substantiation in primary Nahua or Toltec historical sources. These modern interpretations often misrepresent the authentic Aztec figure of the *nahualli*—the practitioner and their animal co-essence.

The Nahualli in an Aztec Framework

The concept of an animal co-essence or spiritual double is not exclusive to the Aztecs; similar beliefs can be found among other Mesoamerican peoples, such as the Wayob of the Maya. This guide, however, is intentionally and precisely focused on the *nahualli* and the transformative path of *nahuallotl* as understood within Aztec metaphysics.

The journey, rituals, and cosmology detailed in this book are drawn directly from verifiable Nahua sources that document Aztec belief. The trials of Mictlan, the distinction between Tlalticpac and Teotl's Mystery, the function of deities like Tezcatlipoca and Xolotl, and the central role of the sacred calendar, the *tonalpohualli*, are all elements grounded in specific Aztec records, such as the *Florentine Codex* and the *Codex Borgia*.

This focused approach is not intended to dismiss the profound wisdom of other traditions. Rather, it is chosen to provide the modern seeker with a clear, deep, and authentic map into the specific, demanding, and ultimately liberating path of the Aztec *nahualli*.

Glossary

- **Apanohuayan** (Dark River)
  A liminal boundary between *tlaltipac* (earthly realm) and *Mictlan* (underworld), symbolising the threshold crossed in *tlahuia* (trance) during initiation (*The Hollowing*).
  Reference: *Florentine Codex*, Book 3.

- **Cemilhuitl** (One Day)
  A single day in the *tonalpohualli* (ritual calendar), used to time rituals and mark spiritual moments across all parts.
  Reference: *Codex Borbonicus*.

- **Chicnauhnepaniuhcan** (Crossroads)
  A spiritual convergence point for decision-making or protection rituals, significant in *The Guide* for leading others.
  Reference: *Florentine Codex*, Book 5.

- **Cihuateteo** (Spirits of Women Who Died in Childbirth)
  Sacred spirits invoked for protection and courage, guiding souls to *Tonatiuh Ilhuicatl*, relevant in *The Hollowing* and *The Guide*.
  Reference: *Florentine Codex*, Book 6.

- **Copal** (Resin Incense)
  Sacred incense burned for purification and connection to *teotl* (divine energy), used in rituals across all parts.
  Reference: *Florentine Codex*, Book 2.

- **Huehuetque** (Ancestral Spirits)
  Ancestral spirits providing guidance and strengthening *tonalli* (life force), invoked in *The Hollowing* and *The Guide*.
  Reference: *Florentine Codex*, Book 6.

- **Ihiyotl** (Spirit/Breath)
  The animating force tied to the liver, balanced during transformation in *The Movement*.
  Reference: *Florentine Codex*, Book 10.

- **Ilhuicatl Yohualli** (Celestial Beings)
  Star spirits influencing *tonalli* during cosmic events, relevant to timing rituals in *The Movement*.
  Reference: *Florentine Codex*, Book 7.

- **Itzcuintli** (Dog)
  A day sign tied to Xolotl, symbolising the Nagual's *nahualli* (spiritual double), prominent in *The Hollowing*.
  Reference: *Codex Borgia*.

- **Limpia** (Cleansing Ritual)
  A purification rite using *copal* and chants to restore *tonalli* and *yolia*, central to *The Guide*.
  Reference: *Florentine Codex*, Book 6.

- **Malinali** (Twisting Energy)
  A spiraling force of renewal driving transformation, key to *The Movement*.
  Reference: León-Portilla, *Aztec Thought and Culture*.

- **Mictlan** (Underworld)
  The realm of the dead, accessed in *tlahuia* to shed attachments (*The Hollowing*).
  Reference: *Florentine Codex*, Book 3.

- **Nahualli** (Spiritual Double)
  The animal co-essence (e.g., dog) tied to one's birth sign, awakened in *The Hollowing* and harnessed throughout.
  Reference: *Florentine Codex*, Book 10.

- **Nepantla** (In-Between)
  A state of being 'in-between,' where one navigates dualities like *Tlalticpac* and *Teotl's Mystery*, fostering transformation (Maffie, 2014). See Part 2 and Part 3, Chapter 15.

- **Ome Yohualli**: A *tonalpohualli* day sign meaning 'Two Nights,' linked to duality and introspection, a time to face one's shadow-self (*Codex Borgia*, 1993). See Introduction and Chapter 17.

- **Olin** (Movement)
  The principle of cyclical change propelling the Nagual's journey, central to *The Movement*.
  Reference: León-Portilla, *Aztec Thought and Culture*.

- **Omeyocan** (Place of Duality)
  The highest heaven of *Ometeotl*, symbolising unity of dual forces, referenced in *The Guide*.
  Reference: *Florentine Codex*, Book 7.

- **Teotl** (Divine Energy)
  The sacred force permeating all things, channeled by the Nagual across all parts.
  Reference: León-Portilla, *Aztec Thought and Culture*.

- **Teyolia**: A heart-centered animistic force tied to vitality and divine connection, persisting after death in *Mictlan*. *Reference: Florentine Codex:* Book 10. See also the Introduction and Part 1.

- **Tezcatlipoca** (Smoking Mirror)
  Deity of fate and sorcery, invoked at *chicnauhnepaniuhcan* (crossroads) in *The Guide*.
  Reference: *Florentine Codex*, Book 1.

- **Tlahuia** (Trance)
  A visionary state for communing with sacred realms, foundational in *The Hollowing*.
  Reference: Inferred from *Florentine Codex*, Book 2.

- **Tlaltipac** (Earthly Realm)
  The material world transcended yet grounded in the Nagual's work, relevant across all parts.
  Reference: *Florentine Codex*, Book 7.

- **Tlamatini** (Wise One)
  The Nagual as a guide interpreting signs and leading rituals, emphasised in *The Guide*.
  Reference: *Codex Mendoza*.

- **Tlatlatzalo** (Banishing Ritual)
  A rite to clear negative forces (e.g., malevolent *ihiyotl*), used in *The Guide*.
  Reference: *Florentine Codex*, Book 6.

- **Tonalpohualli** (Ritual Calendar)
  The 260-day calendar for divining fate and timing rituals, used across all parts.
  Reference: *Codex Borbonicus*.

- **Tonalli** (Life Force/Fate)
  Vital energy tied to birth, purified and aligned throughout the Nagual's journey.
  Reference: *Florentine Codex*, Book 4.

- **Tonatiuh Ilhuicatl** (Heaven of the Sun)
  The solar heaven where *Cihuateteo* guide souls, referenced in protective rites (*The Guide*).
  Reference: *Florentine Codex*, Book 6.

- **Tzitzimime** (Star Demons)
  Malevolent entities threatening *tonalli* during cosmic disruptions, countered in *The Movement*.
  Reference: *Florentine Codex*, Book 7.

- **Xiuhpohualli** (Solar Calendar)
  The 365-day solar cycle, used with *tonalpohualli* for broader transformations (*The Movement*).
  Reference: *Codex Borbonicus*.

- **Xolotl** (Deity of Transformation)
  The skeletal dog deity guiding souls through *Mictlan*, tied to *nahualli* in *The Hollowing*.
  Reference: *Codex Borgia*.

- **Yolia** (Breath/Soul)
  The soul force in the heart, awakened and balanced across the Nagual's path.
  Reference: *Florentine Codex*, Book 10.

Refrences

Aguilar-Moreno, M. (2007). *Handbook to life in the Aztec world*. Oxford University Press.

Boone, E. H. (2007). *Cycles of time and meaning in the Mexican books of fate*. University of Texas Press.

Carrasco, D. (1990). *Religions of Mesoamerica: Cosmovision and ceremonial centers*. Waveland Press.

Codex Borbonicus. (1991). (Facsimile edition, commentary by A. Anders, M. Jansen, & L. R. Reyes). Fondo de Cultura Económica.

Codex Borgia. (1993). (Facsimile edition, commentary by K. A. Nowotny). Dover Publications.

Codex Magliabechiano. (1983). (Facsimile edition, commentary by E. H. Boone). University of California Press.

Codex Mendoza. (1992). (Facsimile edition, commentary by F. F. Berdan & P. R. Anawalt). University of California Press.

Codex Vaticanus A (Codex Rios). (1979). (Facsimile edition, commentary by F. Anders). Akademische Druck- und Verlagsanstalt.

Maffie, J. (2014). *Aztec philosophy: Understanding a world in motion*. University Press of Colorado.

Sahagún, B. de. (1950–1982). *Florentine Codex: General history of the things of New Spain* (A. J. O. Anderson & C. E. Dibble, Trans.). School of American Research and University of Utah Press. (Original work published 16th century)

Index

A

Apanohuayan 25, 26, 27

Aztec Philosophy 73, 105

C

Chalchihutlicue 76, 77, 78, 87, 88, 98

Chicome Coatl 35, 36, 37, 39, 40, 43, 44

Chiconahuapan 29, 30, 31

Codex Borgia 11, 13, 73, 74, 85, 87, 105

Codex Borbonicus 105

Codex Magliabechiano 105

Codex Mendoza 105

Codex Vaticanus A 105

Cozcacuauhtli 21, 23, 24, 33

D

Dream-Work 82, 99

F

Florentine Codex 11, 12, 13, 17, 85, 87, 89, 105

I

Itzcuintlan 7, 17, 18, 19

Iztapaltépetl 37, 38, 39

J

Jade River Flow 88, 98

M

Maffie, James 73, 105

Mictlan 11, 12, 13, 17, 18, 19, 20, 21, 22, 23, 24, 25, 26, 27, 29, 30, 31, 85, 86, 95, 96 (selected pages)

Mictlantecuhtli 76, 77, 78, 85, 86, 88, 95, 96

N

Nahualli 11, 12, 13, 17, 18, 19, 82, 83, 89, 90, 91, 93, 94, 99, 100, 101, 102, 103, 104 (selected pages)

Nahuallotl 11, 12, 13, 73, 74, 75, 76, 77, 78, 79, 80, 82, 83, 84, 85, 86, 87, 88, 89, 90, 91, 93, 94, 95, 96, 97, 98, 99, 100, 101, 102, 103, 104 (selected pages)

O

Obsidian Mirror-Work 84, 94

Ome Yohualli 39, 40, 41, 43, 44, 45, 99

P

Psychopomp Journey 85, 86, 88, 95, 96

Q

Quetzalcoatl 76, 77, 78, 86, 87, 88, 96, 97

R

Rain's Elemental Connection 87, 97

S

Sahagún, B. de 11, 12, 13, 17, 85, 87, 89, 105

Serpent's Creative Offering 87, 96, 97

Shapeshifting 82, 83, 95, 98, 99

T

Teotl 11, 12, 13, 17, 18, 19, 20, 21, 22, 23, 24, 25, 26, 27, 29, 30, 31, 68, 69, 70, 73, 74, 75, 76, 77, 78, 79, 80, 82, 83, 84, 85, 86, 87, 88, 89, 90, 91, 93, 94, 95, 96, 97, 98, 99, 100, 101, 102, 103, 104 (selected pages)

Teotl's Mystery 11, 12, 13, 17, 18, 19, 20, 21, 22, 23, 24, 25, 26, 27, 29, 30, 31, 68, 69, 70, 73, 74, 75, 76, 77, 78, 79, 80, 82, 83, 84, 85, 86, 87, 88, 89, 90, 91, 93, 94, 95, 96, 97, 98, 99, 100, 101, 102, 103, 104 (selected pages)

Tepetl Monamictlan 11, 12, 21, 22, 23, 24

Tlalticpac 11, 12, 13, 17, 18, 19, 20, 21, 22, 23, 24, 25, 26, 27, 29, 30, 31, 68, 69, 70, 73, 74, 75, 76, 77, 78, 79, 80, 82, 83, 84, 85, 86, 87, 88, 89, 90, 91, 93, 94, 95, 96, 97, 98, 99, 100, 101, 102, 103, 104 (selected pages)

Tonalpohualli 12, 13, 99

Tonalli 11, 12, 13, 17, 18, 19, 20, 21, 22, 23, 24, 25, 26, 27, 29, 30, 31, 68, 69, 70, 73, 74, 75, 76, 77, 78, 79, 80, 82, 83, 84, 85, 86, 87, 88, 89, 90, 91, 93, 94, 95, 96, 97, 98, 99, 100, 101, 102, 103, 104 (selected pages)

X

Xolotl 7, 8, 9, 17, 18, 19, 20, 21, 22, 23, 24, 25, 26, 27, 29, 30, 31, 76, 77, 78, 85, 86, 88, 95, 96, 98, 99, 100, 101, 102, 103, 104 (selected pages)

Y

Yolia 17, 82, 89, 99

About the author

Born under the Aztec day sign 4 Dog (Nahui Itzcuintli), **Ty Weston** is a Nahualli Guide on the path of Nahuallotl. Following more than forty years of spiritual exploration, his work is now dedicated to this ancient wisdom, helping people embrace the unknown and recognize the inherent nature that exists in all of us, beyond societal conditioning. He teaches that the *nahualli*—our true spiritual essence—is more real than the illusory world we look at every day.

His writing, including *Entering the Void*, serves as a map for those called to journey through the underworld of the psyche (*Mictlan*) to dissolve illusions and uncover their authentic self.

Based in North Texas, Ty offers sacred services from this ancient lineage. To learn more about Tonalpohualli readings, Tonalli Retrieval, or to book a session, visit him at **www.darkness-whisperer.com**.

www.ingramcontent.com/pod-product-compliance
Lightning Source LLC
Chambersburg PA
CBHW071952070426
42453CB00012BA/2162